Betty Crocker's
NEW
Boys and Girls
COOKBOOK

Illustrated by Gloria Kamen

GOLDEN PRESS

NEW YORK

Dear Boys and Girls,

Learning to cook can be an adventure—like exploring a new country, with a recipe for your map. And if you follow directions exactly, you are sure to arrive at your destination—proud and pleased to be able to cook many good things for your family and friends.

Twenty-five girls and boys, just your age, selected and tested all the recipes and food ideas that you find in this book. From ice cream sodas to Pizzaburgers, from Animal Pancakes to Mad Hatter Meatballs, here are all of the foods they liked best to prepare _and_ to eat.

We hope that you will have a wonderful time with this book—making treats for snacks and parties, beautiful cakes for birthdays, and sometimes even surprising Mother and Dad by cooking supper all by yourself!

Good luck and happy cooking,

Betty Crocker

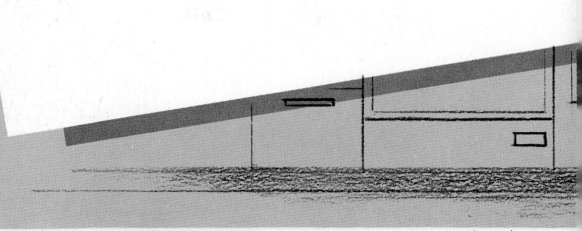

Meet Betty Crocker's Test-Helpers

Betty Crocker's first cookbook for boys and girls appeared in 1957. The recipes in it were very carefully chosen and tested, first in the Betty Crocker Kitchens and then by a panel of 12 boys and girls your age. They cooked in their own kitchens, and only the recipes they liked best and found easy to follow were printed in the book.

The book became so popular that we decided to produce this new and larger revised edition. The new recipes for this book were tested by another group of test-helpers.

We'd like you to meet all the boys and girls on both panels who helped plan this book especially for you. Just turn the page.

Betty Crocker's
Test-Helpers
1957

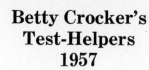

"It's important to measure exactly. When we didn't, we had trouble."—**Lucy**

"We had to say if we liked these dishes enough to make them again."—**Eric**

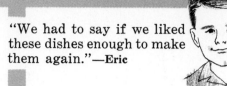

"If I were a Mama, I'd cook all day."—**Elizabeth**

"We learned what words like *baste* and *fold* and *beat* mean."—**Peter**

"Our mothers scored what we made as excellent, good, fair, or poor."—**Linda**

"We had to say if things were easy or difficult and if they tasted good."
—**Bette Anne**

"Being a home-tester was the most exciting thing I've ever done."—**Randee**

"After all the recipes were tested, we had a wonderful party."—**Becky**

"We always said what we thought, even if it wasn't complimentary."—**Ricky**

"If we didn't like it, Betty Crocker didn't put it in this book."—**Chris**

"It's really easy to cook, if you do what the recipe says."—**Eileen**

"We tested about 136 recipes and we liked almost every one of them."—**Donna**

...And here are the new Test-Helpers

"It's important to read all the way through the recipe before you start to cook."
—Joel

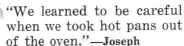

"I learned how to use a sharp knife — without cutting myself."—Sandra

"We learned to be careful when we took hot pans out of the oven."—Joseph

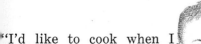

"When I started testing recipes, I didn't know a tablespoon from a teaspoon. Now I know."—Shelley

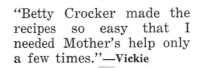

"Betty Crocker made the recipes so easy that I needed Mother's help only a few times."—Vickie

"We always left the kitchen clean. Then Mother liked to have us help."—Alpha

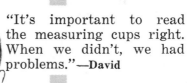

"It's important to read the measuring cups right. When we didn't, we had problems."—David

"I'd like to cook when I grow up, too."—Michael

"Sometimes our best friends helped us decide if we liked the recipe."—Joan

"Mother showed me how to cut parsley and put it on top of soup. It looked pretty there."—Mary Sarah

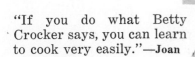

"Betty Crocker is like a real friend to me now."—Carol

"If you do what Betty Crocker says, you can learn to cook very easily."—Joan

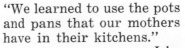

"We learned to use the pots and pans that our mothers have in their kitchens."
—John

Contents

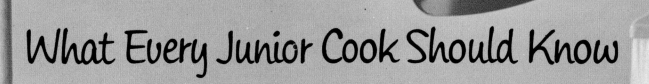

What Every Junior Cook Should Know

Cooking is a skill, just like swimming or riding a bike. It's easy when you learn the correct and safe way from the beginning. So, before you begin, read these important rules and cooking tips. Then follow them always for fun and success in the kitchen.

You'll Want to Know
These Cooking Terms

Bake—Cook in oven.

Beat—Mix vigorously over and over with a spoon or fork, or round and round with a beater.

Blend—Mix thoroughly two or more ingredients until smooth.

Boil—Cook in steaming liquid in which bubbles break on surface.

Broil—Cook directly under heating unit in range, or over hot coals.

Chop—Cut into pieces with knife or chopper.

Cube—Cut into ¼- to ½-inch squares.

Cut in—Mix fat into a flour mixture with a pastry blender, a fork, or two knives.

Dice—Cut into very small ¼-inch squares.

Dot—Drop bits of butter or cheese here and there over food.

Drain—Pour off liquid.

Flour—Dust greased pans with flour until well coated on bottom and sides. Shake out extra flour.

Fold—Mix gently, bringing rubber scraper down through mixture, across bottom, up and over top until blended.

Garnish—Decorate with pieces of colorful food such as parsley, pimiento, cherries, or lemon.

Grate—Rub against grater to cut into small pieces.

Grease—Spread bottom and sides of pan with shortening.

Knead—Work dough with your hands by repeating a folding-back, pressing-forward, and turning motion.

Melt—Heat until liquid.

Mince—Chop or cut into tiny pieces.

Panfry—Cook in small amount of fat in skillet.

Pare—Cut off outside skin, as from an apple or potato.

Peel—Pull off outer skin, as from an orange or banana.

Roll out—Flatten and spread with a rolling pin.

Shred—Cut into very thin strips.

Sift—Put through flour sifter or fine sieve.

Simmer—Cook in liquid almost to boiling but not hot enough to bubble.

Stir—Mix round and round with spoon.

Toss—Mix lightly.

Whip—Beat with rotary egg beater or electric mixer to add air.

Before You Start to Cook

Choose a time to suit your mother, so you won't be in her way.

Be sure to wash your hands.

Wear an apron to keep your clothes clean.

Read your recipe and all the directions in it very carefully.

Put all your ingredients on a tray. Then set aside each one as you use it.

On another tray, put all the utensils and pans you'll need.

When You're Through Cooking

Have you left anything out? Read your recipe again to make sure.

Is everything spic and span? Then your mother will be glad to have you cook again.

Kitchen Safety

It pays to be careful!

Always use pot holders to avoid burns.

When you use the vegetable parer, always cut away from yourself.

Ask your mother before you use a sharp knife, the can opener, or the electric mixer.

Pans won't upset and spill if handles are turned toward back of range.

When you slice, dice, chop, or mince, use a chopping board.

For Preparation

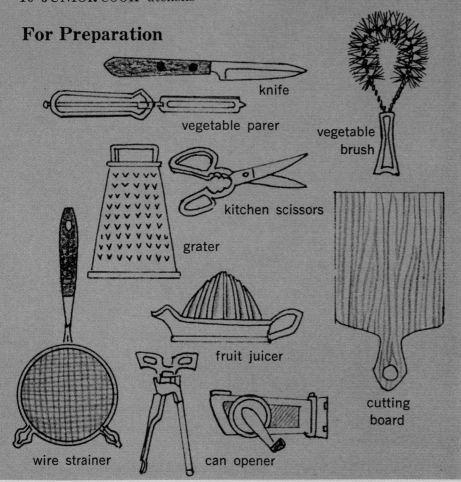

knife

vegetable parer

vegetable brush

kitchen scissors

grater

fruit juicer

cutting board

wire strainer

can opener

For Top-of-Range Cookin

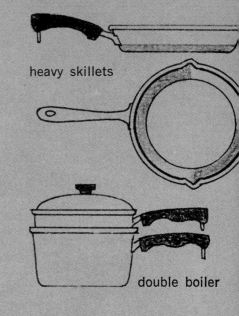

heavy skillets

double boiler

Utensils You

For Measuring

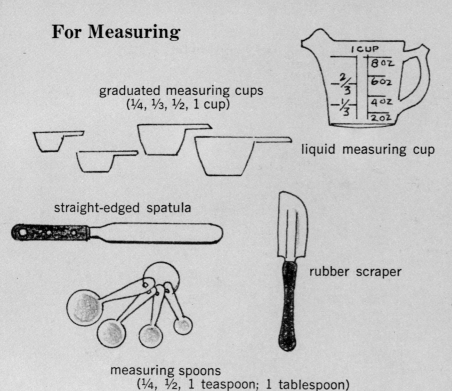

graduated measuring cups
(¼, ⅓, ½, 1 cup)

liquid measuring cup

straight-edged spatula

rubber scraper

measuring spoons
(¼, ½, 1 teaspoon; 1 tablespoon)

For Baking

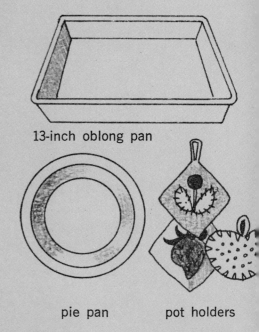

13-inch oblong pan

pie pan

pot holders

For Mixing

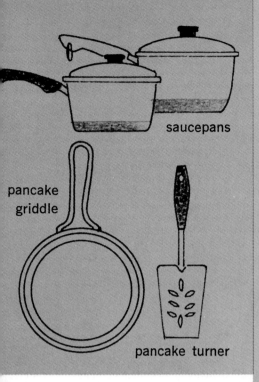

saucepans

pancake
griddle

pancake turner

Nill Need

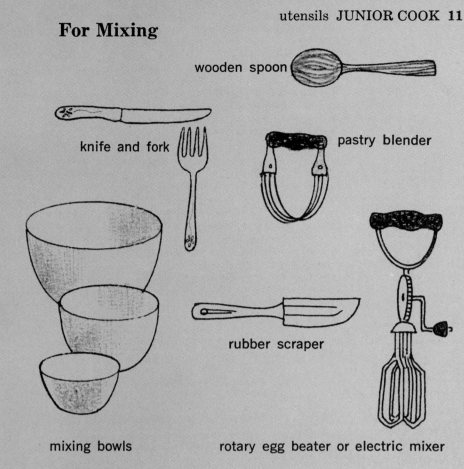

wooden spoon

knife and fork

pastry blender

rubber scraper

mixing bowls

rotary egg beater or electric mixer

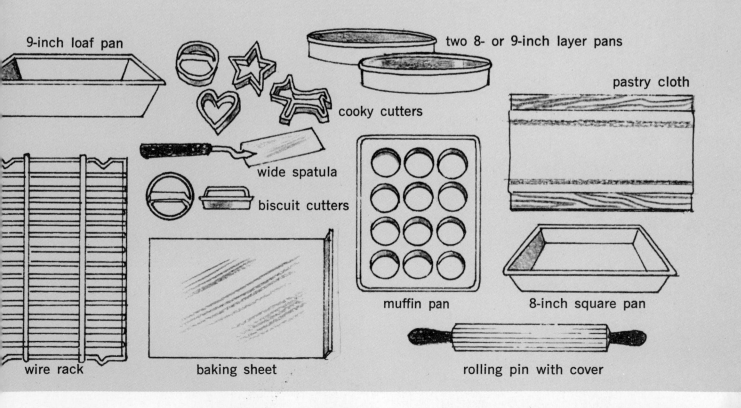

9-inch loaf pan

cooky cutters

two 8- or 9-inch layer pans

pastry cloth

wide spatula

biscuit cutters

muffin pan

8-inch square pan

wire rack

baking sheet

rolling pin with cover

Use Nested-type Measuring Cups for:

Flour—You may use either Gold Medal Regular or Gold Medal Wondra in any recipe in this book calling for Gold Medal Flour. To measure, dip dry measuring cup into flour sack or canister to get it heaping full. Level off with straight-edged spatula or back of table knife. Do not tap cup or pack flour.

When using Gold Medal Wondra Flour, you may pour flour directly from the sack into the cup and level off.

(¼, ⅓, ½, and 1 cup sizes)

White sugar (granulated or confectioners')—(Sift confectioners' sugar before measuring.) Dip dry measuring cup into sack or canister to get it heaping full. (Spoon confectioners' sugar into cup.) Level off with straight-edged spatula or back of table knife. Do not tap cup.

BROWN SUGAR ↗

SUGAR

Brown sugar—Fill dry measuring cup and press down with back of spoon to pack brown sugar firmly. Sugar should hold its shape when turned out of cup.

Shortening, butter, or margarine—Take small amounts with rubber scraper and pack into nested measuring cup. Level off. It's easy to know how much butter or margarine to use if you remember:

1 stick=½ cup   ½ stick=¼ cup

Cut-up foods (such as bread crumbs, chopped celery, onions, or nuts)—Pack lightly into measuring cup until level with top.

Measures Exactly

Use a Liquid-type Measuring Cup for:

Liquids (such as milk, water, or vegetable oil) Place measuring cup on table. Pour in liquid to proper mark. Bend down and look at mark at eye level to be sure it is right.

Use Measuring Spoons for:

($\frac{1}{8}$*, $\frac{1}{4}$, $\frac{1}{2}$, 1 teaspoon, and 1 tablespoon sizes)

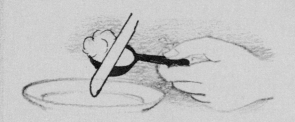

Shortening, butter, or margarine—To measure small amounts, pack into measuring spoon. Level off with straight-edged spatula or back of table knife.

Salt—Pour salt into small glass or bowl and dip into it with a spoon to measure. (Or you may dip into salt stored in small canister.) Level off.

Baking powder, soda, cornstarch, or spices— Stir to loosen the powder in can. Then fill measuring spoon heaping full. Level off.

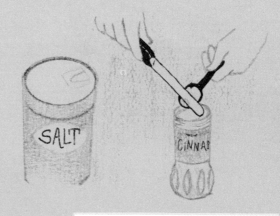

Vanilla — Pour into measuring spoon from bottle. Hold spoon over custard cup or small bowl rather than mixing bowl, to avoid spilling in too much.

***Note:** To measure $\frac{1}{8}$ teaspoon, fill a $\frac{1}{4}$ teaspoon measuring spoon half full.

Kitchen Arithmetic

3 teaspoons = 1 tablespoon

4 tablespoons = $\frac{1}{4}$ cup

8 tablespoons = $\frac{1}{2}$ cup

16 tablespoons = 1 cup

2 cups = 1 pint

2 pints (4 cups) = 1 quart

Setting the Table

For pleasant family meals, set the table as carefully and attractively as you would for company.

Always have a centerpiece—garden flowers, fruit, a little pot of ivy from the window sill, or a figurine from the cupboard shelf.

Arrange silverware in the order in which you use it, with the piece to be used first on the outside, farthest away from the plate. Place forks, napkins, and salad plates at the left; knives, spoons, and glasses at the right.

Fun at Dinnertime

Dinner is the sociable meal of the day when all the family gathers around the table together, and everyone tells what happened at school, at work, and at play.

- Let everyone have a turn at talking. If you must interrupt, say "Excuse me."

- Be interested in what the others have to say.

- Talk about happy subjects.

- Sometimes play a game like Table Topics. Each member of the family takes a turn choosing the topic; then everyone, in turn, tells all he knows about it.

Good Manners at Mealtime

Being polite and considerate is always important. Use your company manners every day. Mealtime is happier for everybody when you remember these rules.

- Wait to begin eating until Mother is seated and all the family has been served.

- Ask for what you want; don't reach. And asking with a "Please" and "Thank you" is the best way of all.

- Keep elbows and arms off the table while you are eating.

- With your knife, cut food into bite-sized pieces, one at a time, to eat it. Break bread or roll into pieces and butter each one as you eat it.

- When you have finished, place knife and fork together across the top of your plate, never with handles resting "gangplank" fashion on the table.

- Use your napkin to blot your lips. At the end of the meal, place it unfolded at the left of your plate.

- Wait until everyone has finished before you ask to be excused from the table. When you are, tell Mother "Thank you."

Beverages

Shake or stir them, beat or heat them—it's like having a soda fountain at home when you can make cool fruit drinks, sodas, shakes, and hot chocolate in your own kitchen. Then serve them with fancy trims or drinking straws for snacks or party treats.

Party Lemonade

Mix in pitcher

½ cup sugar
½ cup hot water

Add

juice of 2 to 3 lemons
½ lemon, thinly sliced
1 quart (4 cups) cold water
12 ice cubes

Stir vigorously with a wooden spoon and pour into tall glasses.

4 servings.

Pink Lemonade

Add a drop of red food coloring or maraschino cherry juice to Party Lemonade.

"We had a circus party with Pink Lemonade and Clown Cupcakes."
—*Randee*

To juice fruits: Cut them in half and place cut side down on the point of a fruit juicer. Pushing down, slowly twist the fruit.

From left to right: Sunny Sipper, Pink Lemonade, Strawberry Cooler, Fruit Float,
Double Lime Cooler, Pink Lemonade, Sunny Sipper

Sunny Sipper

A good and good-for-you drink.

Blend in medium-sized bowl

    ¼ cup honey
    ½ cup orange juice
    juice of 1 lemon

Add

    1 can (6 ounces) evaporated milk
    1 can (12 ounces) apricot nectar

Beat with rotary egg beater until foamy.

Chill in refrigerator.

Beat again before serving.

4 servings.

Lemon-Strawberry Punch

Try this when you want "plenty of punch."

Empty into punch bowl

    3 cans (6 ounces each)
      frozen lemonade concentrate

Dilute with water as directed on cans.

Stir in

    1 package (10 ounces)
      frozen strawberries, thawed

Just before serving, add

    1 quart ginger ale, chilled
    1 small tray of ice cubes

32 servings (about 1 gallon).

Fruit Float

Fill tall glass with — fruit, such as raspberries, blueberries, banana slices, strawberries, or any fruit you like

Pour in — chilled ginger ale

Top with — 1 scoop lime sherbet

1 serving.

Double Lime Cooler

Stir in bowl to soften — ½ pint (1 cup) lime sherbet

Stir in — 1 can (6 ounces) frozen limeade concentrate
2 bottles (7 ounces each) ginger ale, chilled
2 cups water

Pour into glasses.
4 servings.

Red Rouser

Place in tall glass — 1 scoop vanilla ice cream

Fill glass with — chilled bottled cranberry juice

1 serving.

Chocolate Milk Shake

Pour into shaker ═══════════

> 2 cups cold milk
> ¼ cup chocolate sauce
> (canned or bottled)

Add ═══════════

> 2 scoops vanilla ice cream

Cover shaker and shake vigorously.

2 servings.

If you don't have a shaker, use a 1-quart screw-top jar; fasten lid tightly and shake.

Be careful when you open a can. It's very easy to cut yourself on sharp edges.

Chocolate Soda

Mix in tall glass

> **2 tablespoons chocolate sauce (canned or bottled)**
> **¼ cup chilled club soda**

Add

> **1 or 2 large scoops vanilla ice cream**

Fill glass with

> **chilled club soda**

Stir to blend slightly and serve.

1 serving.

Blushing Pink Soda

Mix in tall glass

> **2 tablespoons crushed strawberries**
> **2 tablespoons canned crushed pineapple**
> **2 tablespoons vanilla ice cream**

Stir in

> **¼ cup chilled strawberry soda**

Place in glass almost to the top

> **additional spoonfuls of vanilla ice cream**

Do not pack the ice cream down.

Pour in slowly

> **additional chilled strawberry soda**

1 serving.

Banana-Orange Frosted

Peel and slice

1 ripe banana

Place in bowl and mash with fork.

Add

½ cup orange juice

Beat with rotary egg beater until smooth.

Add

½ cup cold milk
½ pint (1 cup) orange sherbet

Beat again until smooth. Pour into two tall glasses.

Top drinks with

scoops of orange sherbet (½ pint)

Decorate each glass with an orange slice and a banana slice, if you like.

2 servings.

Grape Float

You can make a fancy float with any of your favorite bottled sodas.

Place in tall glass

1 scoop vanilla ice cream

Fill glass with

chilled grape soda

1 serving.

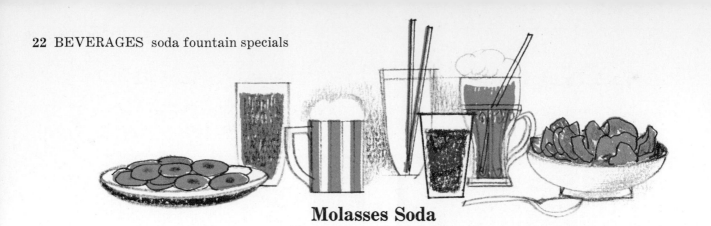

Molasses Soda

Mix in tall glass	1 tablespoon molasses ½ cup cold milk
Add	1 scoop vanilla ice cream
Fill glass with	chilled club soda

1 serving.

Root Beer Float

Some folks call this drink a "black cow."

Place in tall glass	1 scoop vanilla ice cream
Fill glass with	chilled root beer

1 serving.

Fancy-flavored Milks

Choc-o-Nut Milk: In each 8-ounce glass, mix 1 tablespoon peanut butter and 1 tablespoon chocolate syrup with fork. Slowly stir in cold milk.

Honeysuckle Nectar: For each 8-ounce glass of cold milk, use 1 tablespoon honey and 1 tablespoon of your favorite fruit juice concentrate—orange, grape, lemonade, or limeade. Slowly stir the honey and fruit juice into the milk.

Woodsman's Refresher: For each 8-ounce glass of cold milk, use 1 tablespoon maple syrup. Stir the syrup into the milk. Sprinkle lightly with cinnamon.

Cheery Cherry Drink: For each 8-ounce glass of cold milk, use 2 tablespoons maraschino cherry juice. Stir the juice into the milk, and then drop a maraschino cherry "surprise" into each glass.

Jack Frost Warmer

A drink to warm you up after sledding or ice skating.

Stir together in 2-quart saucepan

> **1 quart apple juice or apple cider**
> **¼ cup brown sugar (packed)**
> **5 whole cloves**
> **1 cinnamon stick**

Heat slowly over low heat 15 to 20 minutes.

Remove cloves and cinnamon stick.

Serve warm in mugs topped with orange slices, if you like.

4 servings.

Cocoa Continental

Pictured below with Cinnamon Puffs (page 144).

Blend in saucepan

> **2 tablespoons cocoa**
> **3 tablespoons sugar**
> **⅛ teaspoon salt**

Stir in

> **½ cup hot water**

Bring to boiling over low heat and boil 2 minutes, stirring constantly.

Stir in

> **2 cups milk or 1 cup evaporated milk and 1 cup water**

Heat over low heat—do not boil.

Drop a marshmallow into each cup and pour hot cocoa over it. Or you can serve cocoa with a stick of peppermint candy or topped with whipped cream tinted pink with food coloring.

4 servings.

Tricks with Trimmings

Make good things to drink taste even better!

Floaters

Whipped Cream: Top hot cocoa, an ice cream soda, or a milk shake with a spoonful of sweetened whipped cream. Sprinkle lightly with ground cinnamon or nutmeg, chocolate candy shot, or toasted coconut.

Tinted Ice Cubes: Mix 2 tablespoons maraschino cherry juice or a few drops food coloring with the water in an ice cube tray. Freeze.

Flavored Ice Cubes: Fill ice cube tray with lemonade, orange juice, or other fruit juice instead of water. Freeze.

Fruit Cut-ups: Garnish fruit drinks with floating lemon or lime wedges, orange slices, and sprigs of fresh mint.

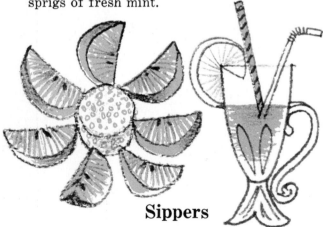

Sippers

Colorful Straws: Serve a cold drink with two or three brightly colored plastic drinking straws. Push straws through pineapple chunks and strawberries, if you like.

Fancy Marshmallows: Pour ¼ cup milk into cup. Place 2 tablespoons tiny colored decorator candies in second cup. Dip marshmallow in milk, then roll in candies. Dry on waxed paper. Push two drinking straws through marshmallow and serve in cold drink.

Hangers

Fruit Slices: Wash and slice a lemon, orange, or lime. Make a cut in each slice from center through peel. Hang over rim of glass.

Fruit Clusters: Separate washed green grapes into tiny clusters by clipping the stem with scissors. Hang one cluster over rim of glass.

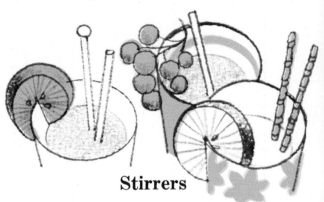

Stirrers

Flavorful Sticks: Serve hot cocoa or cold milk drinks with a stick of cinnamon or peppermint candy in each.

Fruit Kabobs: Serve cold fruit drinks with a fruit kabob in each. To make kabobs, spear two or more pieces of fruit on a wooden pick. Choose from these fruits: maraschino cherries, pineapple chunks, mandarin orange sections, orange wedges, fresh strawberries.

Frosty Glasses

Pour ¼ cup fruit juice (lemon, orange, grape, or cranberry) into shallow bowl. Place ¼ cup granulated sugar on a piece of waxed paper. Hold each glass at the bottom; dip rim of glass into fruit juice, then into sugar. Set glasses upright in refrigerator to chill ½ hour, or until sugar "frost" dries.

Breads and Sandwiches

Pancakes or Pizzaburgers—you'll find recipes for both in this chapter, along with lots of other quick and easy breads and sandwiches. Why not bake muffins or biscuits for breakfast some Saturday soon? And plan to serve Sloppy Joes the next time a friend stays for lunch.

Streusel-topped Rolls

Heat oven to 400°.

Mix with fork in a small bowl

> 2 tablespoons soft butter
> 1/3 cup sugar
> 2 tablespoons flour
> 1/2 teaspoon cinnamon

This mixture is called a streusel mixture.

Remove rolls from

> 1 package (12) brown and serve rolls

Place on a baking sheet.

Spread generously over top of rolls

> soft butter

Spread streusel mixture on rolls.

Bake *6 to 8 minutes,* or until golden brown.

Makes 12 rolls.

Note: Be sure to use *soft* butter in this recipe. It will make the mixing easier.

Nut Bread

Heat oven to 350°.

Grease and flour a loaf pan, 9x5x3 inches.

Measure into large mixer bowl

> 2½ cups Gold Medal Flour
> 1 cup sugar
> 3½ teaspoons baking powder
> 1 teaspoon salt
> 3 tablespoons salad oil
> 1¼ cups milk
> 1 egg
> 1 cup chopped nuts

Beat on medium speed 30 seconds.

Pour into prepared pan.

Bake *55 to 65 minutes,* or until a toothpick stuck in center comes out clean.

Cool. Always slice with a bread knife.

"Betty Crocker said not to worry about a crack in your nut bread. It's supposed to be there."
—Chris

Butterball Coffee Cake

Heat oven to 375°.

Grease a round layer pan, 9x1½ inches.

Melt in small saucepan —————————— | ¼ cup butter

Mix in bowl —————————— | ¾ cup sugar
1 tablespoon cinnamon

Prepare Rolled Biscuits (page 31) as directed except—roll dough ¼ inch thick and cut 18 biscuits with a 2¼-inch cutter.

Dip each biscuit into melted butter, then roll in the cinnamon-sugar mixture.

Place 15 of the biscuits around the outer part of the pan, overlapping to make a circle. Arrange the remaining 3 biscuits to fill the center of the pan. Pour any leftover melted butter over the biscuits.

Sprinkle biscuits with —————————— | ¼ cup chopped nuts

Bake *25 to 30 minutes.*

Allow to stand 5 minutes before serving.

9 servings.

Dip biscuits first into melted butter, then roll in cinnamon mixture.

Overlap the biscuits in the pan like this.

Whirligig Cinnamon Rolls

Sweet and spicy, and so pretty.
Perfect for a Sunday breakfast.

Heat oven to 425°.

Grease 12 muffin cups.

Prepare dough for rolled Biscuits as directed on Bisquick package.

With lightly floured cloth-covered rolling pin, roll dough into a rectangle, 12x7 inches.

Spread with

soft butter

Sprinkle with mixture of

¼ cup sugar
1 teaspoon cinnamon

Beginning at the long side, tightly roll up dough.

Seal by pinching edge into roll.

Cut into 1-inch slices.

Place each slice, cut side down, in muffin cup.

Bake *10 to 15 minutes,* or until brown.

Makes 12 rolls.

"Kneading dough is just like playing with clay — only you can bake dough into something that's good to eat."
—Michael

Your dough will be soft after stirring with fork.

Knead dough by folding over, pressing down, and turning.

Roll dough on floured cloth-covered board.

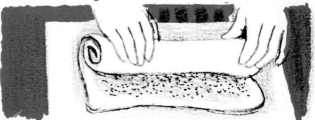

Roll up from the long end of the rectangle.

Place in muffin cups like this.

Butter Sticks

Serve these with your dinner of Simple Spaghetti (page 74).

Heat oven to 450°.

Melt in small saucepan ══════════════════ | ¼ **cup butter**

Pour half of the butter into a square pan, 9x9x2 inches.

Prepare Rolled Biscuits (page 31) as directed except—after kneading, divide dough into 10 parts.

Roll each part between your hands until it is about 9 inches long.

Place biscuit sticks in prepared pan. Pour rest of butter over sticks.

Sprinkle with ══════════════════ | **sesame seed or poppy seed or celery seed**

Bake *18 minutes*.

After removing pan from oven, allow butter sticks to stand in pan about 2 minutes to absorb the butter.

Makes 10 butter sticks.

Drop Biscuits

Heat oven to 450°.

Grease a baking sheet.

Stir together in a bowl —————————

2 cups Gold Medal Flour
3 teaspoons baking powder
1 teaspoon salt

Cut into flour mixture with a pastry blender or two knives ———————

¼ cup shortening

Mixture should be crumbly.

Stir in with a fork ———————

1 cup milk

Stir just until mixture holds together and forms a ball.

Drop tablespoonfuls of dough onto prepared baking sheet. Leave a 2-inch space between biscuits so they will brown nicely.

Bake *10 to 12 minutes*, or until golden brown.

Makes about 20 biscuits.

Rolled Biscuits

Heat oven to 450°.

Set out baking sheet but do not grease.

Follow recipe for Drop Biscuits (page 30) except—*decrease the amount of milk to ¾ cup.* Stir in with a fork just until mixture holds together and forms a ball.

Turn dough onto lightly floured cloth-covered board. Roll ball of dough around 3 or 4 times. Knead quickly and lightly by folding, pressing, and turning. (See page 28.) Repeat this 20 times to smooth up the dough.

With lightly floured cloth-covered rolling pin, roll out dough to ½-inch thickness.

Use a round cutter to cut out biscuits; dip cutter into flour before cutting each biscuit. Cut biscuits close together.

Use a spatula to place biscuits on ungreased baking sheet. For crusty sides, place biscuits about 1 inch apart; for soft sides, place biscuits close together in an ungreased round layer pan.

Bake *10 to 12 minutes,* or until golden brown. Serve hot.

Makes sixteen 1¾-inch biscuits.

Muffins

A muffin is a quick bread baked in the shape of a cupcake.

Heat oven to 400°.

Grease bottoms only of 12 medium-sized muffin cups.

Stir together in bowl

2 cups Gold Medal Flour
¼ cup sugar
3 teaspoons baking powder
1 teaspoon salt

Make a "well" in center of the mixture.

Beat slightly with fork in another bowl

1 egg

Stir in

1 cup milk
¼ cup vegetable oil
   or melted shortening

Pour egg mixture all at once into "well" in flour mixture. Stir *just* until flour is moistened. Batter will be slightly lumpy. *Do not overmix.*

Fill muffin cups ⅔ full.

Bake *20 to 25 minutes*, or until golden brown.

Makes 12 medium-sized muffins.

Whiz Muffins: You can mix up muffins in minutes with our packaged muffin mixes.

Surprise Muffins

Make Muffins (above) except—fill muffin cups only half full of batter. Drop a teaspoonful of jelly in center of batter. Add more batter to fill muffin cups ⅔ full. Discovering the jelly inside the baked muffins is the surprise!

Toast Toppers

Everyone loves crisp, hot buttered toast, even more when it's topped with something sweet or spicy.

Cranberry or Jelly

Spread hot buttered toast with jellied cranberry sauce or currant jelly or orange marmalade. Sprinkle with confectioners' sugar.

Cinnamon Mix

Mix 2 tablespoons sugar and 1 teaspoon cinnamon. Sprinkle on hot buttered toast. Cut toast into strips.

Caramel Coconut

Stir together 2 tablespoons brown sugar, 2 tablespoons flaked coconut, and 1 tablespoon soft butter. Spread on unbuttered toast and place under broiler until "topper" bubbles. Watch carefully.

Raisin-Peanut Butter

Mix ¼ cup peanut butter, 2 tablespoons chopped seedless raisins, and 2 tablespoons orange juice. Spread on hot buttered toast. Cut toast into 2 triangles.

Doughnut Treat

Great for breakfast or an after-school snack.

For each serving, cut a doughnut in half crosswise. Toast doughnut halves, cut side up, under broiler. Watch carefully. Place two toasted halves on a serving plate; spread with orange marmalade. Sprinkle with crisp bacon bits.

Silver Dollar Pancakes

Rolled Pancakes

Branded Pancakes

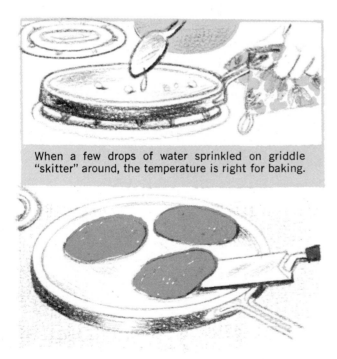

When a few drops of water sprinkled on griddle "skitter" around, the temperature is right for baking.

With a pancake turner, turn pancakes when bubbles appear on top and edges appear somewhat dry.

Pancakes

America's favorite way to start the day.

Prepare batter for Pancakes as directed on Bisquick package.

Lightly grease and heat a heavy skillet or griddle.

Use a 1/4 cup measuring cup as a dipper to pour batter onto hot griddle.

Bake, turning once.

Serve hot with butter and warm syrup.

Note: For thinner pancakes, add more milk; for thicker pancakes, add more Bisquick.

Makes about 18 pancakes.

Basic Pancakes

Animal Pancakes　　　　　　　　*Butterfly Pancakes*

Branded Pancakes

Real Western—with your own brand right on the pancake.

Prepare batter for Pancakes as directed on Bisquick package. Trickle batter from a teaspoon onto hot griddle, forming an initial. (Initials must be made backwards to be right when pancakes are served; so before you start, practice drawing your initial backwards on a piece of paper for a pattern.)

When bottom side of initial has lightly browned, pour about ¼ cup of batter over the initial.

Bake until bubbles appear and edges are slightly dry. Turn and finish baking pancake.

Serve your "brand" hot with butter and warm syrup or jelly.

This is how some letters look backwards.

Put very little batter in your spoon when making the initials.

Animal Pancakes

Prepare batter for Pancakes as directed on Bisquick package.

Form simple animal designs by pouring batter for round pancake onto hot griddle; then with a spoon, add small amounts of batter for ears, tail, feet, etc.

Bake, turning pancakes once.

Bake up a whole "zoo" of pancakes.

Silver Dollar Pancakes

Prepare batter for Pancakes as directed on Bisquick package.

Spoon batter, a tablespoonful at a time, onto hot griddle to form tiny "silver dollar" pancakes. Bake as for other pancakes.

Pile up a high stack for each serving.

Make sure you keep the pancakes small—they're more fun this way.

Butterfly Pancakes

Bake Pancakes as directed on Bisquick package.

To serve, cut pancakes through center. Place curved sides together to resemble a butterfly. Place a sausage in center. Dot pancake "wings" with jelly, if you like.

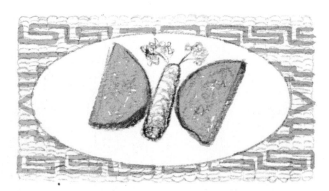

This is the way the butterfly will look.

Rolled Pancakes

Bake Pancakes as directed on Bisquick package.

While warm, spread pancakes with bright red jelly. Roll up.

Serve two or three on each dessert plate.

Sprinkle with confectioners' sugar.

Spread jelly thin. Then roll up like this.

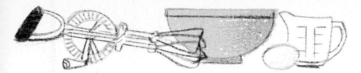

Blueberry Pancakes

Place blueberries from our wild blueberry muffin mix in a strainer over a bowl and let drain. Save blueberry liquid.

Rinse the blueberries with cold water; set aside to drain.

Blend in bowl

> 1 egg
> 1 cup milk

Add

> dry muffin mix from wild
> blueberry muffin mix

Beat with rotary egg beater until well blended.

Fold in

> drained blueberries

Lightly grease heavy skillet or griddle; heat.

Use a ¼ cup measuring cup as a dipper to pour pancake batter into skillet.

With pancake turner, turn pancakes when tops are bubbly and somewhat dry at the edges.

Serve warm with Blueberry Syrup (below).

Blueberry Syrup

Stir together in small saucepan

> blueberry liquid (drained from can)
> ¾ cup maple-flavored syrup

Heat 5 minutes.

To Make Your Pancakes Special

Honey Butter

Beat with rotary egg beater in small bowl until smooth and fluffy

> ½ cup soft butter

Gradually beat in

> ½ cup honey

Cinnamon-Maple Syrup

Stir together in small saucepan and heat 5 minutes

> 1 tablespoon butter
> 1 cup maple-flavored syrup
> ½ teaspoon cinnamon

Red Hot Syrup

Place in small saucepan over low heat

> ½ cup water
> 2 tablespoons red cinnamon candies

Heat until candies have melted, stirring occasionally.

Remove saucepan from heat and slowly stir in

> ½ cup light corn syrup

French Toast

Beat in bowl with rotary egg beater

> 2 eggs
> ½ cup milk
> ¼ teaspoon salt

Cut in half

> 6 slices slightly dry bread

Heat a lightly greased heavy skillet or griddle.

Pick up bread with fork and dip both sides into egg mixture.

Place bread slices in hot skillet or on griddle.

Brown on both sides, turning with pancake turner.

Serve hot. Sprinkle with confectioners' sugar. Top with butter and your favorite syrup or jelly.

6 servings.

Egg Salad Sandwich Rolls

Mix in bowl

3 hard-cooked eggs (page 77), chopped
¼ cup finely chopped celery
½ teaspoon minced onion
3 tablespoons mayonnaise
¼ teaspoon salt

Split

4 sliced frankfurter rolls

With a fork, scoop out center from each half. Fill with egg salad.

Makes 8 sandwiches.

Tea Party Sandwiches

Ribbon Sandwiches

With knife, trim crusts from

2 slices white bread
2 slices whole wheat bread

Mix in small bowl

3 tablespoons shredded process American cheese
3 tablespoons soft butter

Spread cheese-butter mixture on 3 slices of bread. Put the 3 slices together, cheese sides up, alternating slices of white and whole wheat bread. Top with the fourth slice of bread. Press slices firmly together.

Wrap sandwiches with clear plastic wrap or aluminum foil and chill in refrigerator for several hours.

To serve, remove wrap and cut sandwich into 4 slices.

Makes 4 tea sandwiches.

Pinwheel Sandwiches

With knife, trim crusts from

4 slices thin-sliced white bread

Spread each slice with

softened butter, and then pimiento cheese spread

Roll up each slice, fasten with toothpicks, and wrap in clear plastic wrap or aluminum foil.

Chill in refrigerator for several hours.

To serve, remove wrap and cut each roll crosswise into 4 slices.

Makes 16 tea sandwiches.

 **Silhouette Sandwiches**

Butter on one side	**8 slices bread**
Top buttered bread with	**8 slices cold luncheon meat**
Top meat with cut-outs from	**4 slices process American cheese**

To make cut-outs: With a cooky cutter, cut out shape of diamond, heart, dog, or any other design from the center of slice of cheese.

Place cut-out piece of cheese on one sandwich. Put the rest of the slice of cheese on the other sandwich—the meat shows through the space in the cheese, making a silhouette of the cut-out.

Makes 8 open-face sandwiches.

Three-in-One Sandwiches

1

With knife, trim crusts from — **6 slices white bread**

Butter one side of each slice.

Mix in small bowl —
1 hard-cooked egg (page 77), chopped
¼ cup deviled ham
1 tablespoon pickle relish

Spread 3 bread slices with filling. Top with remaining slices to make sandwiches.

2

With knife, trim crusts from — **6 slices whole wheat bread**

Butter one side of each slice.

Place on each of 3 slices — **1 slice process American cheese**

Top with remaining bread slices to make sandwiches.

3

With knife, trim crusts from — **6 slices white bread**

Butter one side of each slice.

Mix in small bowl —
⅓ cup peanut butter
4 slices bacon, crisply cooked and crumbled
1 tablespoon pickle relish

Spread 3 bread slices with filling. Top with remaining slices to make sandwiches.

Cut each of the above sandwiches in half.

Put together a half of *each* kind of sandwich. You will then have three kinds of filling in a complete sandwich.

For a picnic, wrap each sandwich in waxed paper.

Makes 6 sandwiches.

Tuna Burgers

Heat oven to 350°.

Mix in bowl

> 1 can (6½ ounces) tuna
> 1 cup chopped celery
> ½ cup cut-up process American cheese
> 1 small onion, minced
> ¼ cup mayonnaise
> salt and pepper to taste

Spread with soft butter

> 6 split hamburger buns

Fill buns with tuna mixture.

Wrap in aluminum foil and place on baking sheet.

Bake *15 minutes.*

Makes 6 sandwiches.

Western Sandwich

A cowboy's standby.

Melt in small skillet

> 1 tablespoon butter

Add

> ¼ cup minced onion
> 2 tablespoons minced green pepper

Fry slowly until onion is yellow, stirring occasionally. Remove from heat.

Break into bowl

> 4 eggs

Stir in

> ½ cup cubed cooked ham
> ¼ cup milk
> ½ teaspoon salt
> ¼ teaspoon pepper

Beat with a fork. Pour egg mixture into skillet and cook over low heat.

Cook slowly, turning gently with broad spatula as mixture starts to set at bottom of pan. When eggs are cooked through but are still moist and shiny, spoon between slices of bread or hot buttered toast.

Makes 4 sandwiches.

"*We had Tuna Burgers for Sunday supper. I made them in the morning, wrapped each in aluminum foil, and left them in the refrigerator. Then we just heated them at suppertime.*"—Peter

Grilled Cheese Sandwich

For each sandwich, butter generously	**2 slices bread**
Place between bread slices	**1 slice process American cheese**

Lightly spread outside of sandwich with soft butter. Brown lightly on both sides in skillet or on griddle (over low heat) until cheese melts and bread is lightly browned.

Watch carefully! Don't hurry! Sandwich will burn if heat is too high.

Skillet Pizza-wich

For each sandwich, place on 1 slice bread	**1 slice process American cheese**
Spread with	**1 tablespoon canned tomato paste**
Cover with	**1 slice bologna or summer sausage**
Sprinkle lightly with	**crushed oregano**
Top with	**1 slice process American cheese** **1 slice bread**

Lightly spread outside of sandwich with soft butter.

Brown lightly on both sides in skillet or on griddle (over low heat) until cheese melts and bread is lightly browned.

California Burger

Frank Round-up

Pigs-in-Blankets

Hamburgers

Mix thoroughly ——————————

> **1 pound ground beef**
> **¼ cup evaporated milk**
> **1 teaspoon salt**

Form into 4 thick or 8 thin patties.

Heat in skillet ——————————

> **about 1 teaspoon fat**

Place patties in skillet. Fry about 6 to 8 minutes over low heat; turn and fry 6 to 8 minutes more. Do not flatten patties while cooking as this presses out the meat juices.

Serve in warm buttered hamburger buns.

4 servings.

Grilled Frankfurters

Sloppy Joe

Cheeseburger

Cheeseburgers

Fry hamburger patties as directed on page 44. When second sides are browned, remove skillet from heat; top each patty with a thin slice of cheese. To melt cheese, cover skillet and let stand a few minutes. Serve in buttered toasted buns. If you like, make a face on top of buns with pimiento-stuffed olive slices, pickle slices, pimiento strips, and parsley.

Pizzaburgers

Make Cheeseburgers as directed above except— top cheese with a spoonful of heated canned pizza sauce.

California Hamburgers

Butter and toast split hamburger buns or slices of round bread; spread with mayonnaise, if you like. Place lettuce and cooked hamburger (page 44) in bun. Top with onion and tomato slices. Replace bun top.

Double-deckers

For each, cut an unsliced bun in 3 slices. Put a cooked hamburger (page 44) between the bottom and middle slices, then pickle relish and sliced tomato between the middle and top slices.

Sloppy Joes

Heat oven to 325°.

Butter lightly — **6 sliced hamburger buns**

Wrap in aluminum foil and heat in oven *15 minutes*.

Brown in skillet — **1 pound ground beef**

Stir in —
1 can (10½ ounces) tomato soup
1 tablespoon prepared mustard
½ teaspoon salt

Simmer over low heat 10 minutes, stirring occasionally.

Spoon into warm buns.

6 servings.

Frankfurters

Serve in warm buns. Top with your favorite—mustard, catsup, pickle relish.

Simmered Frankfurters

In covered pan, heat 2 cups water to boiling. Drop in frankfurters; lower heat to medium. Cook 5 to 8 minutes.

Grilled Frankfurters

Heat a small amount of fat or oil in a skillet. Cook frankfurters slowly in hot fat, turning them as they brown.

Frank Round-ups

Heat oven to 325°.

Lightly butter

> **4 sliced hamburger buns**

Wrap in aluminum foil and heat in oven *15 minutes*.

Cut across 6 or 7 times, not slicing all the way through

> **4 frankfurters**

Cook frankfurters as directed in recipe for Simmered Frankfurters (above).

Shape each frankfurter in a circle on a warm bun; fill center with mustard and pickle relish.

4 servings.

Coney Island Hot Dogs

Heat oven to 325°.

Lightly butter

> **6 sliced frankfurter buns**

Wrap in aluminum foil and heat in oven *15 minutes*.

Cook 6 frankfurters as directed in recipe for Simmered Frankfurters (left).

Heat in saucepan, stirring constantly

> **1 can (8 ounces) chili con carne**
> **2 tablespoons catsup**

Place a frankfurter in each bun and cover with hot chili mixture.

6 servings.

When cutting frankfurters, be sure not to cut all the way through.

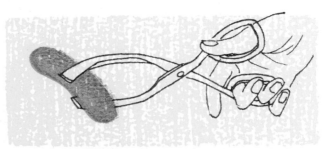

A pair of tongs is very handy for turning and picking up frankfurters.

Pigs in Blankets

Heat oven to 450°

Prepare dough for rolled Biscuits as directed on Bisquick package.

With lightly floured cloth-covered rolling pin, roll out dough into a square, 12x12 inches.

Cut dough into 12 oblong shapes, each 4 inches long and 3 inches wide.

Wrap each oblong around —————————— **1 frankfurter**

The ends of the frankfurter will peek out of the biscuit "blanket."

Place on ungreased baking sheet.

Bake *10 to 15 minutes*.

Serve hot.

Makes 12 sandwiches.

Salads and Vegetables

Be an artist! Make picture-pretty salads that are as tasty as they are attractive. Try your hand at turning radishes into roses. And learn to cook such vegetables as corn on the cob, green beans, and potatoes. You'll find it's twice the fun when *you* choose them at the market.

Crisp Relishes

Fancy little extras like these always look tricky. But they're really easy and fun to make.

Celery Curls

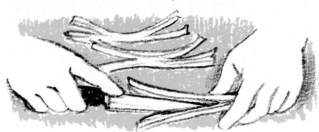

Separate and wash several stalks of celery. Cut stalks into short lengths. (To speed up the job, cut several stalks of celery at once.)

Slit lengths in narrow strips at both ends.

Chill in iced water until ends curl.

Pickle Fans

Make four lengthwise cuts almost to the end of each pickle.

Spread gently to form a little open fan.

Radish Roses

Scrub fresh red radishes. Cut off the root end. Leave a bit of stem and leaf.

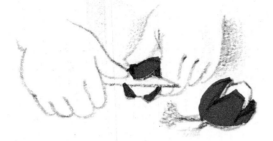

Then, with a small paring knife, cut *thin* "petals" around radish from root end almost to stem end.

Place "roses" in iced water to "blossom." (The cold water makes the radish open its petals.)

Carrot Curls

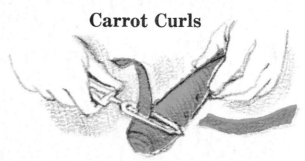

Wash, then pare raw carrots with a vegetable parer. For long, very thin slices, slice the length of carrot paper-thin with parer. Always cut away from your hand.

Roll each slice around your finger, then hold it together with a toothpick.

Chill curls in iced water about an hour so they will hold their shape. Then remove toothpicks.

Crisp Lettuce Leaves

Lettuce is an important part of most salads,
and everyone will want to eat it if it's fresh and crisp.

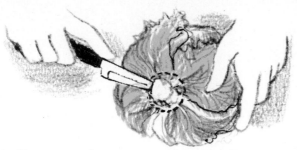

1. To prepare lettuce leaves (called "cups") for a salad, cut out the core of the head with a sharp-pointed knife.

3. Peel off as many leaves as you need and rinse them thoroughly in cold water. Gently pat dry between paper or cloth towels.

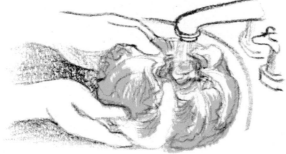

2. To loosen the leaves, hold lettuce, with cut side up, under running water.

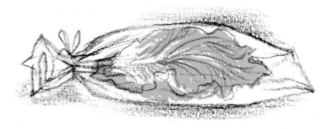

4. Place leaves loosely in plastic bag or wrap in a dry towel. Chill well in the refrigerator.

Speedy Salads on a Plate

Fruit Salads

Serve with a favorite bottled sweet dressing.

Pineapple Chunks 'n Cherries—Arrange drained canned pineapple chunks and pitted dark sweet cherries on lettuce leaves.

Apple and Orange—Alternate slices of unpared apple and orange sections on lettuce leaves.

Grapefruit and Orange—Alternate sections of grapefruit and orange on lettuce leaves.

Banana and Peanuts—Roll slices of banana in finely chopped peanuts; serve on lettuce leaves.

Vegetable Salads

Serve with a favorite bottled tangy dressing.

Tomato and Cucumber—Overlap slices of tomato and unpared cucumber on lettuce leaves.

Lettuce Wedge—Cut head lettuce into small wedges; place each on a salad plate. Pour a little dressing over each. Garnish with one or two radishes or cucumber and tomato slices.

Carrot, Pineapple, and Raisins—Pare raw carrots and slice crosswise, penny-thin. Mix with pineapple tidbits and raisins; stir in a little mayonnaise. Serve on lettuce leaves.

Tossed Green Salad

Wash, dry, and chill —————————— ½ head lettuce

Into a large salad bowl, tear lettuce into bite-sized pieces.

Add —————————————————
½ cup sliced celery
¼ cup sliced radishes
¼ cup sliced carrots

Toss vegetables together with a big salad spoon and fork.

Pour over salad ————————— ¼ cup French Dressing (below)

Toss again until dressing coats all the pieces of vegetables.

Serve immediately.

4 servings.

French Dressing

Find a jar with a tight-fitting cover.

Measure into the jar —————————
½ cup vegetable oil
2 tablespoons vinegar
2 tablespoons lemon juice
½ teaspoon salt
¼ teaspoon paprika
¼ teaspoon dry mustard

Screw on cover securely and shake well.

Keep covered jar of dressing in the refrigerator. Shake dressing again to mix just before using.

Makes ¾ cup.

Note: If you're in a hurry, use bottled French dressing. Or start with an envelope of salad-dressing mix.

Potato Salad

A favorite salad in the summertime.

Boil ———————————————— **4 medium unpared potatoes**

(Use enough water to cover potatoes and 1 teaspoon salt. Cover and cook 30 to 35 minutes, or until skins start to break and fork slips in easily.)

Drain water, then cover potatoes with cold water and drain again. Cool slightly.

Place potatoes on cutting board and pull off skins. (Use a fork to hold potatoes, if you like.) Slice potatoes or cut in cubes. Place in salad bowl.

Sprinkle in ———————————————— **¼ teaspoon salt**

Add ————————————————
**1 cup sliced celery
¼ cup minced onion
¼ cup pickle relish
¼ cup French dressing
3 hard-cooked eggs (page 77), sliced**

Toss gently and chill thoroughly.

Just before serving, fold in ———————— **½ cup mayonnaise or salad dressing**

Serve in lettuce-lined bowl. Trim with more hard-cooked egg slices, if you like.

6 servings.

To mince onions in a hurry: Cut surface of onion in tiny squares; then cut across in thin slices.

Toss salad gently so you won't break the potato and egg slices.

Fruit Basket Upset

Serve as a salad or as a fluffy pink dessert. A favorite with our test panel.

Place in large bowl

> 1 can (8 ounces) fruit cocktail, drained
> 2 bananas, peeled and sliced
> 1 small apple, cut into small pieces
> ½ cup halved seedless green grapes
> ½ cup sliced strawberries, if you like
> 5 maraschino cherries, cut up
> ¼ cup miniature marshmallows

In small bowl, beat with rotary egg beater until stiff

> ½ cup whipping cream

Tint whipped cream with

> 2 teaspoons maraschino cherry juice or 1 or 2 drops red food coloring

Fold whipped cream into fruit.

Spoon salad into serving bowl; trim with fresh strawberries and green grapes.

Refrigerate until ready to serve. Serve with cinnamon toast.

4 to 6 servings.

Waldorf Salad

Cut, core, and dice

> **2 apples (leave red skin on)**

Place in bowl.

Add and lightly toss

> **1 cup sliced celery**
> **a few broken nuts, if you like**

Blend in another bowl

> **¼ cup mayonnaise**
> **2 tablespoons milk**

Then add to apple mixture and toss together.

Serve on crisp lettuce leaves.

4 servings.

How to Dice an Apple

Cut apple in wedges like this. Cut out core and seeds.

Slice each wedge in fourths like this.

Then cut apple slices into squares.

Raggedy Ann Salad

Body

> **fresh or canned peach half**

Arms and legs

> **small celery sticks**

Head

> **large marshmallow**

Eyes, nose, shoes, buttons

> **raisins**

Mouth

> **cut of cherry**

Hair

> **shredded yellow cheese**

Skirt

> **ruffly leaf of lettuce**

Bunny Salad

For each serving, place crisp lettuce leaf on plate.

On top of it, place upside down

> **1 chilled pear half**

Make bunny with narrow end for face.

Eyes

> **2 raisins**

Nose

> **1 red cinnamon candy**

Ears

> **2 blanched almonds**

Tail

> **cottage cheese ball**

Rocket Salad

For each serving, place a crisp lettuce leaf on a salad plate.

Launching pad

> **1 slice pineapple**

Rocket

> **½ peeled banana set upright in center of pineapple slice**

Nose cone

> **½ maraschino cherry fastened to top of banana with a toothpick**

Sunshine Salad

Empty into small bowl ——————— **1 package (3 ounces) lemon-flavored gelatin**

Pour in ——————— **1 cup boiling water**

Stir until gelatin is dissolved.

Stir in ——————— **½ cup cold water**
1 can (8¾ ounces) crushed pineapple
⅛ teaspoon salt

Chill in refrigerator until gelatin starts to thicken.

Meanwhile, pare and grate ——————— **2 medium-sized carrots**

Stir into gelatin.

Pour into a square pan, 8x8x2 inches. Chill in refrigerator until firm.

Cut in squares. Lift out carefully and serve on crisp lettuce leaves. Top with mayonnaise.

6 to 9 servings.

Use a knife to cut salad in squares.

Frozen Vegetables

To cook, follow package directions carefully.

As a rule, do not thaw before cooking. Usually 4 servings per 10-ounce package.

Canned Vegetables

Pour liquid from canned vegetables into saucepan. Boil, uncovered, until liquid cooks down.

Add 1 tablespoon butter and vegetables; heat quickly.

Buttered Green Beans

Wash and snap off ends of 1½ pounds green beans. Place beans on cutting board and cut into 1-inch lengths.

In covered saucepan, heat about 1 inch salted water to boiling.

Add beans and bring to boil, then turn down heat and cook 5 minutes. Then cover pan and cook slowly 10 to 15 minutes or until tender.

Drain any extra water and add 1 tablespoon butter.

4 servings.

Eddie the Eggplant

This is Eddie the Eggplant, made from an eggplant that grew in a strange way. Next time you find an oddly shaped vegetable, see what a funny face you can make!

Corn on the Cob

Just before cooking, remove husks and silks.

In large covered saucepan, heat to boiling enough water to cover corn.

Carefully drop corn into boiling water. Cover and boil 5 to 8 minutes, depending on the size and age of the corn.

A little sugar in the water helps the flavor of older corn.

Scalloped Corn

Heat oven to 350°.

Beat slightly with fork or rotary egg beater in bowl

1 egg

Stir in

1 can (1 pound) cream style corn
½ cup milk
½ cup cracker or bread crumbs
¼ cup chopped onion
1 tablespoon butter
1 teaspoon salt
⅛ teaspoon pepper

Pour corn mixture into 1-quart baking dish.

Bake *35 minutes.*

4 servings.

"Don't worry if the onion makes your eyes water."—Donna

Cabbage Wedges

Remove outer leaves of medium-sized cabbage head. Place on cutting board and cut in half, storing one half for later use.

Turn flat side down and cut in half again.

Once more cut each piece in half to make four wedges. Cut out core in each.

Cook cabbage, uncovered, in enough boiling salted water to cover the wedges. Boil gently 10 to 15 minutes, until tender. Prick with a fork to test.

Drain off water and add 1 tablespoon butter. Turn wedges so they are all buttered.

Serve a wedge to each person. Sprinkle with paprika for color.

4 servings.

This is how you cut the cabbage in wedges.

Flopsy-Mopsy Carrots

See these pictured on page 69.

Remove tops from fresh small carrots; scrub and pare.

Cook, covered, in 1 inch boiling salted water 15 to 20 minutes, or until tender. Add more water if needed. Drain. Dot with butter. To serve: Remove carrots to serving plate, stick stems of parsley into each carrot for "carrot tops."

Black-eyed Susan Carrots

Sugar-glazed carrots arranged around ripe olives look like a gay flower.

Melt in heavy saucepan

2 tablespoons butter

Remove from heat and blend in

¼ cup brown sugar (packed)
2 teaspoons prepared mustard
½ teaspoon salt

Add

1 can (1 pound) small whole carrots, drained

Cover; cook over *low heat* 10 minutes, until carrots are heated through. Stir occasionally.

Place in center of a serving plate

6 to 8 large pitted ripe olives

Remove carrots from sauce with tongs; arrange on plate around ripe olives with the slender tips of the carrots toward the olives. Pour the sauce over the carrots.

4 servings.

Boiled Potatoes

Pare potatoes. In a covered saucepan, heat to boiling enough salted water to cover potatoes. Add potatoes and cook, covered, until tender. It takes about 30 minutes, depending on size of potatoes.

Prick with fork to tell when tender. Drain.

Serve with butter, salt, and pepper . . . and a sprinkling of parsley, if you like.

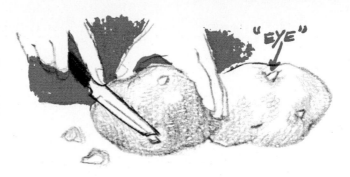

Cut out "eyes" of potato with point of vegetable parer or small knife.

Mashed Potatoes

Pare and quarter —————————— **6 medium potatoes**

In a covered saucepan, heat to boiling enough salted water to cover potatoes. Add potatoes and cook, covered, until tender. It takes about 20 to 25 minutes.

Prick potatoes with a fork to tell when tender.

Drain remaining water. Mash with potato masher.

Add ——————————
**½ cup hot milk
3 tablespoons butter
¼ teaspoon salt**

Beat with electric mixer or spoon until light and fluffy.

4 to 6 servings.

Baked Potatoes

Heat oven to 400°. Choose baking potatoes (the long brown kind) of medium size. Scrub with a brush. To soften skins, rub them with a little butter or shortening. Prick skin with fork to let steam escape during baking.

Bake *about 1 hour*, or until potatoes are soft (prick with fork to test). To serve plain baked potatoes, cut crisscross gash on potato tops. Squeeze until some of potato pops up through opening. Season with salt, pepper, and butter.

Potatoes Anna

Pare | **4 medium potatoes**

Cut in paper-thin slices. Rinse slices with cool water.

Melt in heavy skillet | **2 tablespoons butter**

Arrange slices in two or three layers in skillet, sprinkling each layer with salt and dotting with butter. (You may overlap your potatoes a little, but each layer should be only one slice thick.)

Cover tightly and heat until steaming. Turn heat to low and cook 15 minutes, or until potatoes are tender. Uncover. Cook until the bottom is crispy and brown. Remove skillet from heat.

With knife, cut through layers to divide potatoes into four sections. With pancake turner, turn out each section, browned side up, on serving plate.

4 servings.

Scalloped Potatoes

Heat oven to 350°.

Arrange in four layers in a
2-quart casserole | **4 cups thinly sliced pared potatoes**

Sprinkle each of the first *three* layers with |
1 tablespoon flour
1 tablespoon minced onion
¼ teaspoon salt
dash of pepper

Dot each layer with | **1 tablespoon butter**

Sprinkle top layer with |
1 tablespoon minced onion
¼ teaspoon salt
dash of pepper

Dot with | **1 tablespoon butter**

Pour over all | **2½ cups hot milk**

Bake, covered, *30 minutes.* Uncover; bake *1 hour.*

4 servings.

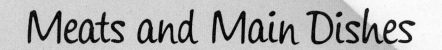

Meats and Main Dishes

Here are recipes for the meats and main dishes that young cooks tell us they like best! First, learn to fix Scrambled Eggs or Macaroni and Cheese; then try Meat Loaf, Simple Spaghetti, Mulligan Stew, and many other favorite mealtime treats.

Meat Loaf

Heat oven to 350°.

Beat slightly in bowl ———————————

1 egg

Add and mix well ———————————

1½ pounds ground beef or meat loaf mixture
3 slices soft bread, torn into pieces
1 cup milk
¼ cup minced onion
1 tablespoon Worcestershire sauce
1¼ teaspoons salt

Place in loaf pan, 9x5x3 inches. Pat evenly to make top smooth.

Bake *1 hour.*

Drain off fat. Turn out of pan.

6 to 8 servings.

Things You Can Do With Meat Loaf

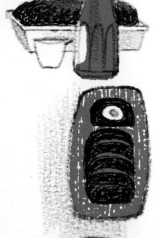

Hot Topper

Spread 3 tablespoons catsup or chili sauce over top of loaf before baking.

Tuckaway Meat Loaf

When forming loaf, tuck 3 shelled hard-cooked eggs down the middle of meat mixture.

Baby Beefies

Shape meat loaf mixture into 8 small loaves and place in shallow pan. Spread catsup or chili sauce over tops of loaves; top each baby loaf with a thin slice of onion. Bake at 350° for *45 minutes.*

Meat Loaf à la Mode

Pictured at right with Buttered Green Peas and Tomato and Cucumber Salad (page 52).

Shape meat loaf mixture into round layer pan, 9x1½ inches. Press a hole in center (to hold excess fat). Pat top of loaf to make smooth. Bake at 350° for *1 hour.*

While meat is baking, prepare Mashed Potatoes (page 61).

To serve, cut meat loaf into 6 pie-shaped wedges. Place each wedge on a plate and top with a scoop of mashed potatoes. Pass butter for potatoes.

"Leftover meat loaf makes the most wonderful sandwiches!"—Becky

Oven-fried Drumsticks

Heat oven to 425°.

Melt in small pan	⅓ cup shortening (part butter)
Mix in paper bag	¼ cup Gold Medal Flour ½ teaspoon salt ⅛ teaspoon pepper ½ teaspoon paprika
Doing three or four at a time, shake in bag to coat with flour	2 pounds chicken legs

Place chicken legs in a single layer in an oblong pan, 13x9½x2 inches. Drizzle melted shortening evenly over the chicken.

Bake *45 minutes*, or until chicken is tender.

4 to 6 servings.

"It was fun to shake the drumsticks in the paper bag."—Vickie

Cube Steaks

Cube steaks are inexpensive cuts of beef, ¼ to ½ inch thick,
cubed by a machine that makes the meat more tender.

Melt in skillet ▬▬▬▬▬▬▬▬▬▬▬▬▬ **2 or 3 tablespoons butter**

(This is just enough butter to keep meat from sticking to pan.)

Dip in flour ▬▬▬▬▬▬▬▬▬▬▬▬▬ **cube steaks**

(The flour keeps juices in the steaks and helps them brown.)

Place steaks in hot skillet and fry one side 4 to 6 minutes, or until browned as you like it.

Turn and fry other side 4 to 6 minutes more.

Remove steaks to hot plate; sprinkle with salt and pepper. If you like, top with squares of butter.

Serve immediately.

"Ham" Loaf Hawaiian

Heat oven to 375°.

Cutting a little more than halfway through,
divide into 8 sections ▬▬▬▬▬▬▬▬▬▬ | **1 loaf (12-ounce can) pork luncheon meat**

Place in a small baking dish.

Starting with the first cut, spread in
every other cut ▬▬▬▬▬▬▬▬▬▬ | **½ teaspoon prepared mustard**

In the same cuts, place ▬▬▬▬▬▬▬▬ | **½ of a pineapple ring**

(If you like, stick whole cloves into the pineapple rings.)

Sprinkle over loaf ▬▬▬▬▬▬▬▬ | **2 tablespoons brown sugar**

Bake *20 minutes.*

To serve, slice through loaf at every other cut so that the pineapple is in the middle of each serving.

4 servings.

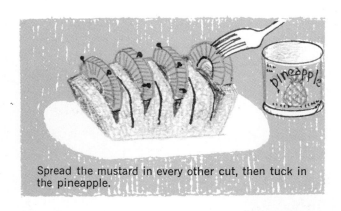

Spread the mustard in every other cut, then tuck in the pineapple.

To serve, cut through loaf like this.

Mad Hatter Meatballs

Have a storybook supper—serve with Flopsy-Mopsy Carrots (page 60)
and fluffy Mashed Potatoes (page 61).

Melt in skillet	**1 tablespoon butter**
Add and cook until tender	**1 green pepper, chopped** **1 onion, minced**
Stir in	**1 can (10½ ounces) chicken with rice soup** **1 can (10½ ounces) tomato soup** **1 cup water**

Heat to boiling. Then turn down heat and simmer sauce, stirring occasionally.

While this sauce cooks, make meatballs.

Beat slightly in bowl	**1 egg**
Add and mix well	**1 pound ground beef** **2 slices soft bread, torn into pieces** **¼ cup evaporated milk** **1 teaspoon salt**

Shape meat into balls about the size of ping-pong balls.

Drop balls into simmering sauce and cook slowly about 1 hour, or until sauce has thickened.

6 servings.

Noodle Goulash

Heat oven to 375°.

Heat in large skillet —————— 1 tablespoon vegetable oil

Add and cook —————— 1 pound ground beef
1 small onion, finely chopped
1 cup diced celery
1 teaspoon salt

Break meat apart with fork and stir as meat browns. Set aside.

Cook as directed on package —————— noodles from 1 package of our
noodles Italiano

Drain the noodles; place in 2-quart casserole.

To the meat mixture, add and mix well —————— contents of tomato sauce mix packet
1½ cups hot water
contents of cheese filling packet

Pour meat mixture over noodles; mix carefully.

Bake *20 minutes.*

Garnish with tomato wedges and sprigs of parsley in the center.

4 to 6 servings.

Drain noodles in a sieve—it's easier this way.

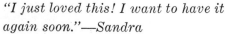

"I just loved this! I want to have it again soon."—Sandra

Tuna and Chips Casserole

Heat oven to 350°.

Empty into 1-quart casserole

1 can (10½ ounces) cream of mushroom soup

Mix in

½ cup milk

Put potato chips between sheets of waxed paper. Crush chips with a rolling pin. Repeat until you have 1¼ cups crushed potato chips.

Drain oil from

1 can (7 ounces) tuna

Add to soup in casserole

drained tuna
1 cup crushed potato chips
1 cup cooked green peas

Mix these ingredients gently.

Sprinkle top with

¼ cup crushed potato chips

Bake *25 to 30 minutes.*

3 to 4 servings.

"It was exciting to make a main dish for supper — and everyone liked it."—Alpha

Polka-dotted Macaroni and Cheese

Heat oven to 375°.

Cook and drain as directed on package —— **1 package (7 ounces) macaroni**

Empty into bowl —— **1 can (10½ ounces) Cheddar cheese soup**

Slowly stir in —— **½ cup milk**
1 teaspoon Worcestershire sauce, if you like

Spread drained macaroni in baking dish, 10x6x1½ inches. Then pour cheese sauce over macaroni, stirring to mix.

Cut into penny-thin slices —— **2 frankfurters**

Arrange frankfurter slices on top of macaroni and cheese.

Bake *25 minutes*, or until mixture is hot and bubbly.

4 to 6 servings.

Lay bacon flat on board to cut across in strips.

Spanish Rice

Prepare as directed on package ———— | **1 cup uncooked white rice**

Heat oven to 400°.

Cut into 1-inch pieces ———— | **4 slices bacon**

Fry bacon in large skillet over medium heat until crisp. Lift bacon out of skillet. Place in 1½-quart casserole.

Stir bacon around to grease casserole.

Add to the bacon fat in skillet ———— | **¼ cup minced onion**

Cook until onion is yellow and soft.

Stir in ———— | **cooked rice (about 3 cups)**
1 can (16 ounces) tomatoes (2 cups)
1½ teaspoons salt

Pour mixture into casserole.

Sprinkle over top ———— | **¼ cup shredded or cut-up process American cheese**

Bake *25 to 30 minutes.*

4 to 6 servings.

Simple Spaghetti

We thank the Italians for this delicious dish, pictured with Butter Sticks (page 29).

Heat in heavy skillet — **1 tablespoon vegetable oil**

Add and cook — **½ cup chopped onion**
½ pound ground beef

Break meat apart with fork and stir as it browns lightly.

Stir in and blend well — **2 cans (8 ounces each) tomato sauce**
1½ cups water
1½ teaspoons salt
1 teaspoon dried parsley
½ teaspoon dried basil
¼ teaspoon pepper

Bring to boiling.

Break in half — **4 ounces uncooked spaghetti (half an 8-ounce package)**

Sprinkle spaghetti into the boiling sauce a little at a time, stirring to keep it separated. Cover tightly. Simmer 20 to 25 minutes, or until just tender, stirring occasionally.

If you like, sprinkle with grated Parmesan cheese.

3 to 4 servings.

Italian Pizza

Brown in small skillet ━━━━━━━━━━━━━━━━━━━━━━━━ ½ **pound ground beef**

Break meat apart with fork and stir as it browns lightly.

Stir in ━━━━━━━━━━━━━━━━━━━━━━━━ ¼ **cup chopped onion**
1 **can (8 ounces) tomato sauce**

Remove from heat.

Heat oven to 425°.

Stir with fork in a bowl ━━━━━━━━━━━━━ 2 **cups Bisquick**
½ **cup water**

Knead dough about 1 minute on lightly floured board. With a lightly floured rolling pin, roll into two 10-inch circles. Place on baking sheets.

Pinch edge of dough to make a slight rim.

Spread half of the sauce mixture on each circle.

Top each with

½ **cup shredded or cut-up mozzarella cheese**

Sprinkle oregano lightly over cheese.

Bake *20 minutes,* or until crust is brown and topping is hot and bubbly.

Cut into pie-shaped wedges and serve immediately.

4 servings.

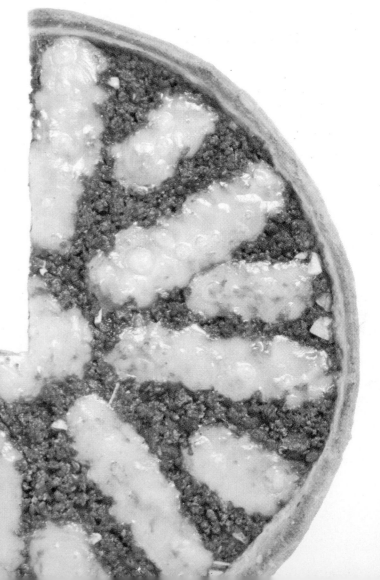

Scrambled Eggs

How much fun to stir egg and milk into fluffy golden mounds!

Break into bowl

2 eggs

Add

2 tablespoons milk
⅛ teaspoon salt

Beat with fork.

Heat in small heavy skillet

1 or 2 teaspoons butter or bacon fat

Tip pan so bottom of pan is completely greased with fat.

Pour in egg mixture. Cook slowly over low heat, turning gently with broad spatula as mixture starts to set at bottom of pan.

Serve when eggs are cooked through, but are still moist and shiny.

1 to 2 servings.

Scrambled Eggs with Cheese

Make Scrambled Eggs (left) except—add 2 tablespoons shredded cheese and ½ teaspoon minced onion to the egg mixture.

Scrambled Eggs with Dried Beef

Make Scrambled Eggs (left) except—add small pieces of dried beef to the hot fat before you add the eggs.

Hard-cooked Eggs

Cover eggs with lukewarm water in saucepan. Heat just until water boils.

Remove pan from heat and cover. Let stand *off heat* just 15 to 18 minutes.

Set saucepan in sink and run in cold water to cool eggs quickly. This makes eggs easier to shell and keeps yolks from turning dark around the edges.

Note: To shell hard-cooked eggs, tap to crack shell. Roll between hands to loosen shell. Hold under cold water as you peel shell.

Soft-cooked Eggs

Never boil eggs. Cook them slowly and gently.

Cover eggs with lukewarm water in saucepan. Heat just until water boils.

Remove pan from heat and cover. Let stand *off heat* 2 to 4 minutes.

Set saucepan in sink and run in cold water for just a few seconds. Be careful not to chill. Break shell by cracking sharply with a knife. Scoop egg from shell with a teaspoon. Serve in a saucedish. Season egg with butter, a sprinkle of salt and pepper.

Fried Eggs

Heat a thin layer of butter or bacon fat in heavy skillet until moderately hot. Break eggs, one at a time, into saucer. Slip into skillet.

Reduce heat to low. Cook slowly, spooning fat over eggs until whites are set and a film forms over yolks, about 3 to 4 minutes. You can turn the eggs, if you like. Cook until yolks are as you want them. Sprinkle with salt and pepper.

It's easier to keep the yolks whole if you slip the eggs one at a time from a saucer into the skillet.

Chili Concoction

This spicy, hearty dish is typical of Mexican cooking. Wonderful for winter parties.

Mix in large heavy kettle

> 1½ pounds ground beef
> 1 cup chopped onion

Break meat apart with fork and stir as it browns lightly.

Stir in

> 1 can (1 pound 12 ounces) tomatoes
> 1 can (6 ounces) tomato paste
> 1 can (15 ounces) kidney beans, drained
> 1 tablespoon sugar
> 2 teaspoons chili powder
> 1 teaspoon salt

Heat to boiling, then lower heat.

Simmer, uncovered, 1 hour, stirring occasionally.

4 to 6 servings.

Mulligan Stew

In the kitchens of Ireland, kettles of hearty stew like this simmer on the range
for hungry children.

Melt in heavy skillet ▬▬▬▬▬▬ | **1 tablespoon shortening**

Add and brown over medium heat ▬▬▬ | **1 pound stewing beef, cut in small pieces**

Add ▬▬▬▬▬▬▬▬▬ | **1 teaspoon salt**

Stir in ▬▬▬▬▬▬▬ | **1 can (10½ ounces) tomato soup**
1 soup can water

Cover tightly and let cook slowly until tender, about 1½ hours.

When meat is tender, add ▬▬▬▬ | **3 carrots, cut in thick slices**
3 potatoes, pared and quartered
3 onions, halved

Cover and continue cooking slowly, about 30 minutes. If there is not enough liquid, add more water during cooking.

If stew is too thin, take off lid and cook sauce until thickened.

4 to 6 servings.

Creamy Chicken-Vegetable Soup

Stir in saucepan until blended ————

> 1 can (10½ ounces) cream of celery soup
> 1 can (10½ ounces) chicken-vegetable soup
> 1 soup can water
> 1 soup can milk

Heat to boiling, then lower heat and simmer 3 to 5 minutes.

4 servings.

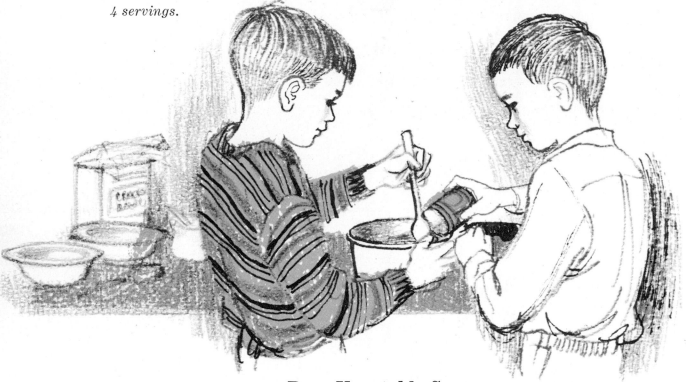

Rosy Vegetable Soup

Remember—soup is best when served piping hot with crackers or bread sticks.

Stir in saucepan until blended ————

> 1 can (10½ ounces) vegetable-beef soup
> ½ soup can tomato juice
> ½ soup can water

Heat to boiling, then lower heat and simmer 3 to 5 minutes.

2 servings.

Cookies, Cakes, and Other Desserts

It's a thrill to bake cookies by the dozen or beautiful cakes. See how quickly they disappear! With the easy-to-follow recipes in this chapter, you can serve your family and guests such company desserts as Strawberry Shortcake, Cherry Tarts, and Hot Fudge Pudding.

Stir-'n-Drop Oatmeal Cookies

Just about the best cooky there is for an after-school snack . . .
with a tall glass of milk.

Heat oven to 375°.

Lightly grease a baking sheet.

Stir together in bowl
— 1 cup Gold Medal Flour
1 teaspoon baking powder
½ teaspoon salt
½ teaspoon cinnamon
½ teaspoon ginger

Add
— 1 cup brown sugar (packed)
1 cup rolled oats

Mix in thoroughly
— ¼ cup vegetable oil
2 tablespoons milk
1 egg

Stir in
— ¾ cup chopped walnuts, if you like

Drop dough by rounded teaspoonfuls about 2 inches apart on baking sheet.

Bake *about 10 minutes*.

Cool on a wire rack.

Makes about 3 dozen cookies.

To grease a baking sheet: Use a piece of waxed paper or paper towel; dip paper in soft shortening, then rub over baking sheet.

Chocolate Chip Cookies

Heat oven to 375°.

Mix thoroughly in bowl

⅓ cup soft shortening
⅓ cup butter
½ cup granulated sugar
½ cup brown sugar (packed)
1 egg
1 teaspoon vanilla

Stir together in another bowl

1½ cups Gold Medal Flour
½ teaspoon soda
½ teaspoon salt

Mix these dry ingredients into the shortening mixture.

Thoroughly work in

½ cup chopped walnuts
1 package (6 ounces) semisweet
chocolate pieces (1 cup)

Drop dough by rounded teaspoonfuls 2 inches apart on ungreased baking sheet.

Bake *8 to 10 minutes,* or until lightly browned but still soft.

Cool on wire rack.

Makes 4 to 5 dozen cookies.

Note: When using Gold Medal Wondra Flour, the dough may look and feel different from what you're used to, just as the flour looks and feels different. Continue on as you normally do (adding more liquid if needed), working with your fingertips until the dough holds together.

Use a rubber scraper to push the cooky dough from the spoon. (It's a good idea to fix the second sheet of cookies while the first one is in the oven.)

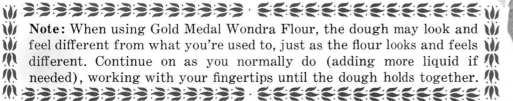

Candy Dandies

These are lots of fun to make—nobody can guess what's in them.

Heat oven to 375°.

Mix thoroughly in bowl

> ¼ cup soft butter
> ¾ cup brown sugar (packed)
> 1 egg

Stir in

> 1⅓ cups Bisquick
> ½ cup chopped nuts
> 1 chocolate-covered coconut candy bar (about 2 ounces), cut up

Drop dough by teaspoonfuls about 2 inches apart on ungreased baking sheet.

Top each cooky with a walnut half, if you like.

Bake *about 10 minutes,* or until lightly browned.

If cookies spread too much during baking, stir a little Bisquick into remaining dough.

Cool on wire rack.

Makes 3 to 4 dozen cookies.

Date Drop Cookies

A quickie with a mix.

Heat oven to 400°.

Lightly grease a baking sheet.

Remove packet of date filling from

Empty packet into bowl.

Stir into date filling

Mix in thoroughly

1 package of our date bar mix
¼ cup <u>hot</u> water
crumbly mixture (from package of date bar mix) **1 egg**

Drop dough by rounded teaspoonfuls about 2 inches apart on baking sheet.

Bake *8 to 10 minutes*.

Cool on wire rack.

Makes about 2½ dozen cookies.

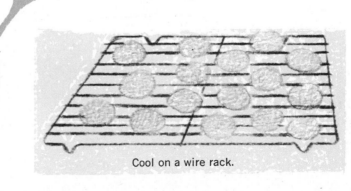

Cool on a wire rack.

Sparkling Sugar Cookies

Just the thing with a glass of lemonade.

Heat oven to 400°.

Lightly grease a baking sheet.

Mix thoroughly in bowl

½ cup soft shortening
1 cup sugar
1 teaspoon grated lemon peel

Blend in

1 egg
2 tablespoons milk

Stir together in another bowl

2 cups Gold Medal Flour
1 teaspoon baking powder
½ teaspoon salt
½ teaspoon soda

Mix these dry ingredients into shortening mixture.

Drop dough by rounded teaspoonfuls about 2 inches apart on baking sheet.

Grease the bottom of a glass. To flatten each cooky, dip glass in sugar and press on dough. For gay cookies, use colored decorators' sugar.

Bake *8 to 10 minutes,* or until a light golden brown.

Cool on wire rack.

Makes about 3 dozen cookies.

Lollipop Cookies

Make dough for Sparkling Sugar Cookies (above). Drop 6 teaspoonfuls of dough far apart on baking sheet; lightly flatten with your fingers. Place 1 popsicle stick, pointing inward, and 1 chocolate mint wafer on each cooky. Top each mint-topped cooky with another teaspoonful of dough. With your fingers, lightly flatten each cooky into lollipop shape. Bake and cool as above.

Salted Peanut Crisps

Heat oven to 375°.

Lightly grease a baking sheet.

Mix thoroughly in bowl
> 1 cup soft shortening (part butter)
> 1½ cups brown sugar (packed)
> 2 eggs
> 2 teaspoons vanilla

Stir together in another bowl
> 3 cups Gold Medal Flour
> 1 teaspoon salt
> ½ teaspoon soda

Mix these dry ingredients into shortening mixture.

Stir in
> 2 cups salted peanuts

Drop dough by rounded teaspoonfuls about 2 inches apart on baking sheet.

Grease the bottom of a glass. To flatten each cooky, dip glass in sugar and press on dough.

Bake *8 to 10 minutes.*

Cool on wire rack.

Makes about 6 dozen cookies.

Flatten cooky with a sugar-dipped glass.

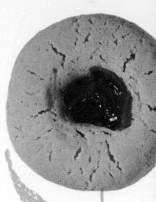

Quick Peanut Butter Cookies

So easy because you start with a cake mix!

Heat oven to 375°.

Mix in large bowl

> ½ package of our yellow cake mix
> 1 cup chunk-style peanut butter
> 2 eggs
> ⅓ cup water

Beat with a spoon or electric mixer until smooth and well blended.

Blend in

> remaining ½ package of our yellow cake mix

Mix thoroughly. (It may be necessary to use your hands to mix the dough.)

Drop dough by teaspoonfuls about 3 inches apart on ungreased baking sheet. (Cookies should be about the size of walnuts.)

With a fork dipped in flour, flatten rounds of dough by pressing a crisscross design on top of each cooky.

Bake *8 to 10 minutes*, or until a light golden brown.

Cool cookies on baking sheet about 2 minutes, then remove to a wire rack to cool.

Makes 4 to 5 dozen cookies.

Peanut Butter and Jelly Cookies

Make Peanut Butter Cookies as directed (left) except—do not flatten cookies with a fork. Make a shallow hole in each cooky by pressing down in the center with the tip of a teaspoon dipped in flour. After baking, place about ½ teaspoon red jelly in each hole.

For Peanut Butter and Jelly Cookies, press tip of a spoon in center. This makes a hole to hold the jelly.

Flatten dough, crisscross style, with a fork dipped in flour.

Molasses Crinkles

Mix thoroughly in bowl

¾ cup soft shortening
1 cup brown sugar (packed)
1 egg
¼ cup molasses

Stir together in another bowl

2¼ cups Gold Medal Flour
2 teaspoons soda
1 teaspoon cinnamon
1 teaspoon ginger
½ teaspoon cloves
¼ teaspoon salt

Mix these dry ingredients into shortening mixture.

Chill dough in refrigerator 2 hours or overnight.

Heat oven to 375°.

Lightly grease a baking sheet.

Roll teaspoonfuls of chilled dough into balls the size of large walnuts.

Dip tops in sugar. Place cookies, sugared side up, 3 inches apart on baking sheet.

Bake *10 to 12 minutes,* or just until set but not hard.

Cool on wire rack.

Makes 4 dozen cookies.

Roll dough into balls the size of large walnuts.

Dip tops in sugar.

Hidden Jewels

Heat oven to 350°.

Grease well an oblong pan, 13x9½x2 inches.

Beat in bowl with rotary egg beater

> **4 egg yolks**

Stir in

> **2¼ cups brown sugar (packed)**
> **1 tablespoon water**
> **1 teaspoon vanilla**

Stir together in another bowl

> **2 cups Gold Medal Flour**
> **1 teaspoon baking powder**
> **½ teaspoon salt**

With kitchen scissors that have been dipped in water, finely cut up

> **1 cup multicolored gumdrops**

Mix the dry ingredients into egg mixture.

Stir in gumdrops and

> **¾ cup chopped walnuts**

Beat in small bowl with rotary egg beater until stiff but not dry

> **4 egg whites**

Stir beaten egg whites into cooky dough.

Spread in prepared pan.

Bake *30 to 35 minutes.*

Cool in pan 20 minutes; cut into bars.

Makes about 3 dozen bars.

Separating an Egg

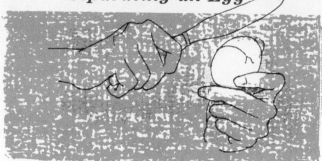

Two bowls are needed—one for the whites, one for the yolks. Crack egg.

With the cracked side on top, pull open shell. Rock the yellow yolk into one half and let the white pour into one bowl.

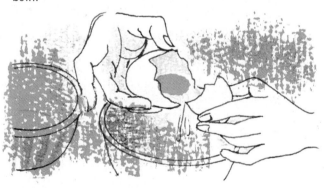

Rock the yolk from one shell to the other until all the white flows into the first bowl.

Drop the yolk into the second bowl. If a bit of yolk falls into the whites, be sure to remove it. Use an edge of the shell to lift it out.

Brownies

Heat oven to 350°.

Grease a square pan, 8x8x2 inches.

In bottom part of double boiler, heat about 1 inch water to boiling.

Place in top part of double boiler

> **2 squares unsweetened chocolate (2 ounces)**
> **⅓ cup shortening**

Set over the boiling water to melt, stirring occasionally.

Remove from heat.

Beat in with rotary egg beater

> **1 cup sugar**
> **2 eggs**

Stir together in bowl

> **¾ cup Gold Medal Flour**
> **½ teaspoon baking powder**
> **½ teaspoon salt**

Mix these dry ingredients into the chocolate mixture.

Stir in

> **½ cup chopped nuts, if you like**

Spread batter in prepared pan.

Bake *30 to 35 minutes,* or until a toothpick stuck into center comes out clean. Cool in pan and cut into squares.

Makes about 16 squares.

Brownie Slowpokes

These are extra good with chocolate frosting.

Heat oven to 375°.

Grease a baking sheet.

Prepare fudgy brownies as directed on package (1 pound) of our fudge brownie mix except—omit nuts.

For each "slowpoke," place 3 walnut or pecan halves (with the ends touching at center) on a baking sheet.

Drop a level teaspoonful of brownie dough in center of each group of nuts.

Bake *10 minutes.*

Cool slightly before removing from baking sheet.

Cool on wire rack.

Makes about 4 dozen cookies.

Paintbrush Cookies

Did you ever "paint" a cooky? Well, you can with Egg Yolk Paint—as bright and beautiful as any artist's colors. Remember these cookies for something to do on a rainy day.

Mix thoroughly in bowl

⅓ cup sugar
⅓ cup soft shortening
⅔ cup honey
1 egg
1 teaspoon vanilla

Stir together in another bowl

2¾ cups Gold Medal Flour
1 teaspoon soda
1 teaspoon salt

Mix these dry ingredients into shortening mixture. Chill dough 1 hour.

Heat oven to 375°. Lightly grease a baking sheet.

Divide chilled dough into 3 portions. (Place 2 portions of dough in refrigerator until ready to use.)

On a lightly floured board, roll out dough with floured rolling pin. Roll to ¼-inch thickness. (For easiest rolling, use a lightly floured cloth-covered board and rolling pin.) Cut into different shapes. (See next page.)

Place on prepared baking sheet. With small paintbrushes, paint designs on cookies with Egg Yolk Paint (below).

Bake *8 to 10 minutes*. For clear colors, do not let cookies brown.

Let cookies cool about 2 minutes on baking sheet, then cool on a wire rack.

Makes about 5 dozen cookies.

Egg Yolk Paint

Blend well in small bowl

1 egg yolk
¼ teaspoon water

Divide mixture among several small custard cups. Add a different food coloring to each cup to make bright colors. If "paint" thickens, add a few drops of water.

Be An Artist—Design Your Own Cooky Shapes

If you have cooky cutters that you like, you will want to use them. Always dip cutter in flour first so that it won't stick to the dough.

It's fun to make your own patterns, too. Just trace these patterns and paste them on heavy cardboard. Cut out each one and grease one side of it. Place pattern, greased side down, on dough and cut around it with a sharp knife. Remove pattern and lift cooky onto baking sheet with wide spatula.

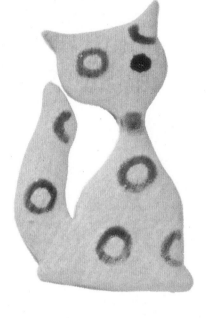

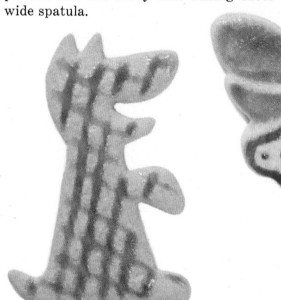

Try your hand at Storybook Cookies, like Peter Rabbit and his carrot, the Gingham Dog and the Calico Cat. Trace pictures from your favorite storybooks to make patterns.

Now you can let your imagination go—see what exciting designs *you* can create.

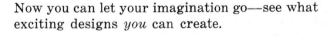

Gingerbread Boys

Mix thoroughly in bowl ——————

> ¼ cup soft shortening
> ½ cup sugar

Mix in ——————

> ½ cup dark molasses
> ¼ cup water

Stir together in another bowl ——————

> 2½ cups Gold Medal Flour
> ¾ teaspoon salt
> ½ teaspoon soda
> ¾ teaspoon ginger
> ¼ teaspoon nutmeg
> ⅛ teaspoon allspice

Mix these dry ingredients into molasses mixture.

Chill dough 2 to 3 hours.

Heat oven to 375°.

Lightly grease a baking sheet.

Divide dough into 3 portions. (Place 2 portions of dough in refrigerator until ready to use.) On a lightly floured board, roll out dough with floured rolling pin. Roll to ¼-inch thickness. (For easiest rolling, use a lightly floured cloth-covered board and rolling pin.)

Cut with a gingerbread-boy cutter dipped in flour.

With wide spatula, carefully place gingerbread boys on prepared baking sheet.

After your little boys are lined up on the baking sheet, add eyes and buttons of raisins, red cinnamon candies, or bits of gumdrops. And for boys that are running, carefully push up a leg on each. Dough arms, turned up at an angle, make boys that wave "hello" as they come out of the oven.

Bake *10 to 12 minutes.*

Cool slightly, then carefully remove from baking sheet. Cool on wire rack.

Make outlines for collar, cuffs, belt, and shoes with Creamy Frosting (page 95).

Makes about 15 Gingerbread Boys.

Speedy Gingerbread Boys

Heat oven to 375°.

Lightly grease a baking sheet.

Mix in bowl until smooth

> **1 package of our gingerbread mix**
> **¼ cup lukewarm water**

Turn out dough onto a lightly floured cloth-covered board.

Knead the dough with your hands until smooth. Roll a small amount of dough at a time. (Keep rest of dough in refrigerator.) Roll to ⅛-inch thickness. Cut with a floured cutter.

With a wide spatula, carefully place the gingerbread boys on prepared baking sheet. Decorate with raisins or red cinnamon candies.

Bake *6 to 8 minutes*. Cool slightly, then carefully remove from baking sheet. Cool on rack.

Outline with Creamy Frosting (below).

Makes 3 dozen Gingerbread Boys.

Creamy Frosting

Mix 1 cup sifted confectioners' sugar, 4 teaspoons milk, and ¼ teaspoon vanilla in small bowl. Tint with food coloring, if you like.

Lumberjack Cookies

See these pictured on page 151.

Make Gingerbread Boy dough as directed above. With a large cooky cutter, or an empty coffee can, cut dough into big circles. Bake and cool as above. Frost cookies with Creamy Frosting tinted your favorite color.

Makes about 15 large round cookies.

Cake Tips for You to Follow

1. How to grease and flour pans:

Use narrow pastry brush or piece of waxed paper to spread soft shortening over inside of pans. Cover both bottom and sides generously.

Put a little flour in greased pan; shake from side to side until flour coats bottom and sides of pan. Tap out extra flour.

2. How to tell when cake is done:

When baking time is up, stick toothpick in center of cake. If it comes out clean, cake is done.

3. How to remove cake from pan:

(Ask Mother to help you with this the first few times.)

Remove cake from oven. Cool in pan on rack 10 minutes. Then place a towel-covered wire rack over top of cake.

Holding racks together with hands, turn cake over. (The towel keeps the wire bars from leaving marks on the cake.) Carefully lift the pan from the cake.

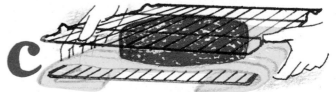

Now, place another wire rack over bottom of cake. Holding both racks together, turn cake right side up to cool. Remove top rack. Notice that it takes 3 racks to remove 2 layers of cake from pans.

4. How to remove large cake from pan:

Some of the cakes on the following pages are baked in large oblong pans, 13x9½x2 inches. Let cake cool in pan 8 to 10 minutes. Then top with a towel and baking sheet; turn over and lift off pan. Place wire rack over bottom of cake. Holding on to baking sheet and rack, turn cake over. Support one end of cake with another rack if needed.

Cocoa Fudge Cake

Heat oven to 350°.

Grease and flour an oblong pan, 13x9½x2 inches.

Stir together in mixer bowl

1⅔ cups Gold Medal Flour
1½ cups sugar
⅔ cup cocoa
1½ teaspoons soda
1 teaspoon salt

Mix in

½ cup soft shortening
1½ cups buttermilk
1 teaspoon vanilla

Beat for 2 minutes at medium speed on electric mixer or 300 strokes by hand. (If you use an electric mixer, scrape the sides and bottom of bowl often with a rubber scraper. But be careful—don't catch the scraper in the beaters.)

Add

2 eggs

Beat 2 minutes more, scraping bottom and sides of bowl often.

Pour into prepared pan.

Bake *40 to 45 minutes.*

Cool in pan on wire rack.

Frost with Quick Fudge Frosting (page 104).

Velvet Crumb Cake

Heat oven to 350°.

Grease and flour a square pan, 8x8x2 inches.

Prepare batter for Velvet Crumb Cake as directed on Bisquick package.

Pour batter into prepared pan.

Bake *about 35 minutes.*

While cake is warm, cover with Broiled Coconut Icing (below).

"Baking is as much fun as my chemistry set. And you can eat what you mix up."
—Eric

Broiled Coconut Icing

Mix in small bowl

> 3 tablespoons soft butter
> ⅓ cup brown sugar (packed)
> 2 tablespoons cream or milk
> ½ cup flaked coconut
> ¼ cup chopped nuts

Spread mixture over warm cake in pan.

Place under broiler until mixture bubbles and browns (3 to 5 minutes). Watch the icing closely as it broils, so it won't burn.

Brownie Fudge Cake

Heat oven to 350°.

Grease a square pan, 9x9x1¾ inches.

Empty into small mixer bowl

> 1 package (1 pound) of our fudge brownie mix

Blend in

> ¼ cup water
> 2 eggs

Beat 1 minute at medium speed on electric mixer or 150 strokes by hand. Scrape sides and bottom of bowl often.

Blend in

> ¼ cup water

Beat 1 more minute, scraping bowl often.

Stir in

> ½ cup chopped nuts

Pour into prepared pan and bake *25 to 30 minutes.*

Cool slightly in pan on rack.

While cake is warm, frost with Easy Cocoa Icing (below).

Easy Cocoa Icing

Mix in small bowl

> 1⅓ cups sifted confectioners' sugar
> ¼ cup cocoa
> ¼ cup soft butter
> 1 tablespoon milk

Stir until well blended. If icing is too stiff, add another tablespoon of milk.

Enchanted Castle Cake

1. Cover a large flat tray or piece of cardboard with aluminum foil for serving tray.*

2. Bake cake batter in oblong pan, 13x9½x2 inches, as directed on ——————— **1 package of our yellow cake mix**

Cool in pan 10 minutes; remove from pan. Cool thoroughly.

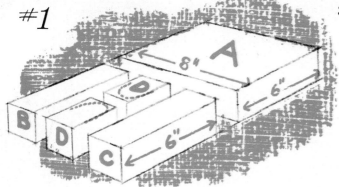

#1

3. Cut cake in following manner (see diagram 1):

- First cut cake in half crosswise into 2 rectangles, 8x6 inches.
- Cut one half into 3 equal pieces, each about 6x2½ inches.
- Cut the center piece in half to make 2 small squares (**D** in diagram 1). With a sharp knife, trim these squares to make the cut edges rounded. These pieces are for the towers.

4. Prepare frosting as directed on ——————— **1 package of our fluffy white frosting mix**

5. Place large cake rectangle (**A** in diagram 1) on foil-covered tray with longer side to the front. Frost top. Place pieces **B** and **C** on top as shown in diagram 2. Spread a thin coating of frosting on all cut sides.
Frost cake completely, making edges as square as possible.

6. Prepare another package of ——————— **our fluffy white frosting mix**

(Use as needed; save leftover frosting to make Marguerites, page 125.)

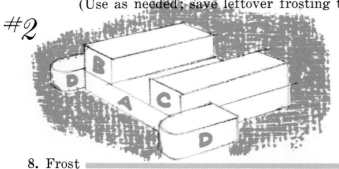

#2

7. Place **D** pieces at the front corners of the cake so that they extend beyond the front edge (see diagram 2). Frost.

8. Frost ——————— **2 pointed ice cream cones**

(Place cones over fingers to frost.)

Sprinkle cones with pink decorators' sugar. Place on top of **D** pieces.

9. Arrange along top edges of castle and towers **pink pillow mints**

10. Break into sections **2 bars (⅞ ounce each) milk chocolate candy**

Trim and place on front and back of castle for windows. (For round windows, trim chocolate squares with sharp knife.) Use chocolate sections for center door and drawbridge. Pink toothpicks can be the chains of the drawbridge.

11. Cut flags from construction paper; fasten with frosting onto toothpicks. Insert in cake and in tips of cones.

*Note: If you like, cover tray or board with blue foil—leave a border of this foil showing around castle for the water in moat. Cover remaining foil with green-tinted coconut "grass," as shown in picture.

"My father took a picture of me with my cake."—Joan

Clown Cupcakes

Bake cupcakes as directed on package of our devils food cake mix. Cool. When ready to serve, cut cone-shaped pieces out of tops of cupcakes.

Fill cavity of each cake with a scoop of vanilla ice cream. Make faces with candies. For peaked hats, place cone-shaped pieces on clown heads.

Button Cake

Bake your favorite layer cake.

Frost cake with

Butter Frosting (page 104)

To decorate, use

flat cream wafer mints of different colors

Using a toothpick, draw a face on each mint with mixture of

**3 tablespoons confectioners' sugar
1 teaspoon milk**

Name Cake

This is a cake that will fit anybody's birthday. You can use our cake mix in your favorite flavor, frost it with Easy Penuche Frosting (page 105) or any light-colored frosting. Spell out the name with semisweet chocolate pieces.

"I made one for Dad's birthday. It was spice cake with caramel fudge frosting and Dad said it was keen."
—*Peter*

To draw faces, use a toothpick.

Frosting Makes the Cake

Frosting is at its best when it is creamy and smooth, but still holds its shape.

When you are going to frost a layer cake—

1. Turn one layer *upside down* on cake plate. Place several spoonfuls of frosting on the layer and spread it to the edge.

2. Place second layer, *right side up,* on frosting.

3. Frost the sides, spreading up from bottom to top with knife full of frosting.

4. Place rest of frosting on top and swirl it around to decorate. Now, aren't you proud?

Quick Fudge Frosting

Mix in saucepan

> 1 cup sugar
> ¼ cup cocoa

Stir in

> ¼ cup butter
> ½ cup milk
> 2 tablespoons light corn syrup

Bring to boiling. Boil for 3 minutes, stirring occasionally.

Remove from heat. Set pan in cold water.

When you can hold your hand on the bottom of the pan, the syrup is cool enough.

Stir in

> 1½ cups sifted confectioners' sugar
> 1 teaspoon vanilla

Stir the frosting until thick enough to spread. If frosting is too thin, add a little more confectioners' sugar. If too thick, add a little more milk.

Makes enough frosting for a round two-layer cake or a big oblong cake or 3 dozen cupcakes.

Whiz Frosting

It takes only a jiffy when you use one of our frosting mixes. You don't even cook it. Just prepare as directed on the package.

Butter Frosting

Blend in bowl

> ⅓ cup soft butter
> 1 cup sifted confectioners' sugar
> 1½ teaspoons vanilla
> 3 tablespoons cream or milk

Stir in

> 2 cups more sifted confectioners' sugar

Beat until frosting is fluffy. If frosting is too thin, add a little more confectioners' sugar. If too thick, add a little more milk.

Makes enough frosting for a round two-layer cake or a big oblong cake or 3 dozen cupcakes.

"Frosting the sides is tricky so I just frost the top. When I get more practice, I'll do the sides, too."
—*Ricky*

Leftover Butter Frosting makes a great filling for graham cracker sandwiches.

Easy Penuche Frosting

Penuche is really candy.

Melt in saucepan ———— **½ cup butter**

Stir in ———— **1 cup brown sugar (packed)**

Cook over low heat for 2 minutes, *stirring constantly.*

Stir in ———— **¼ cup milk**

Bring to a full rolling boil, stirring constantly.

Remove from heat. Set pan in cold water.

When you can hold your hand on the bottom of the pan, the syrup is cool enough.

Blend in ———— **1 ¾ to 2 cups sifted confectioners' sugar**

Put pan in iced water. Beat until thick enough to spread. If frosting is too thin, add more confectioners' sugar. If too thick, add a few drops of hot water.

Candy Fluff Toppings

Serve angel food cake cut in wedges and top with one of the following. Each topping recipe serves 6.

Peppermint Fluff

Whip 1 cup whipping cream. Fold in ½ cup crushed peppermint candy (about 10 penny red and white candy sticks). Spoon on wedges of cake; sprinkle with more crushed peppermint candy.

Note: To crush candy sticks or bars, place them between pieces of waxed paper and crush with a rolling pin.

Rocky Road Fluff

Whip 1 cup whipping cream. Fold in ½ cup salted peanuts and ½ cup multicolored candy-coated milk chocolate candies. Spoon on wedges of cake; sprinkle with more candies.

Chocolate Crunch

Whip 1 cup whipping cream. Fold in 2 crushed chocolate-coated toffee candy bars.

Gingerbread

Heat oven to 325°.

Grease and flour a square pan, 9x9x1¾ inches.

Mix thoroughly in bowl

> ½ cup soft shortening
> 2 tablespoons sugar
> 1 egg

Blend in

> 1 cup dark molasses
> 1 cup boiling water

Stir together in another bowl

> 2¼ cups Gold Medal Flour
> 1 teaspoon soda
> ½ teaspoon salt
> 1 teaspoon ginger
> 1 teaspoon cinnamon

Stir these dry ingredients into molasses mixture.

Beat until smooth.

Pour into prepared pan.

Bake *45 to 50 minutes.*

If you like, spread with Fire Dog Topping (below).

Fire Dog Topping

Mix in a small bowl

> 1 cup sifted confectioners' sugar
> 1 tablespoon milk

Spread over hot gingerbread. Sprinkle top with brown sugar.

Serve warm.

Whiz Gingerbread

For this delicious quickie, prepare as directed on our gingerbread mix package.

Strawberry Shortcake

As good as Grandma's—maybe better.

Heat oven to 450°.

Prepare dough for Fruit Shortcake as directed on Bisquick package.

Lightly flour hands and pat half of dough in an ungreased round layer pan, 8x1½ inches.

Dot with

butter

With lightly floured rolling pin, roll out rest of dough into 8-inch circle and place on top. (For easiest rolling, use a lightly floured cloth-covered board and rolling pin.)

Bake *15 to 20 minutes,* or until nicely browned.

Remove from pan.

To serve, split crosswise while warm.

Spoon between layers and over top

1 quart sweetened fresh strawberries

Serve warm with plain cream or sweetened whipped cream.

6 to 8 servings.

Apple Crisp

A real family dessert. Especially good on a cold winter's night.

Heat oven to 350°.

Spread evenly in square pan, 8x8x2 inches

4 cups sliced pared apples

Sprinkle with

**¼ cup water
1 teaspoon cinnamon
½ teaspoon salt**

With pastry blender, mix until crumbly

**1 cup sugar
¾ cup Gold Medal Flour
⅓ cup soft butter**

Spread crumb mixture over apples.

Bake, uncovered, *about 40 minutes.*

Serve warm with milk or cream.

6 servings.

Rosy Cinnamon Baked Apples

Heat oven to 375°.

Wash and core

4 baking apples

(Have mother help you core the apples.)

Blend in square pan, 9x9x1¾ inches

**1 cup water
¼ cup brown sugar (packed)**

Place apples in pan.

Fill apple centers with

red cinnamon candies

Bake *40 to 45 minutes,* or until apples are tender when pierced with a fork.

Spoon sugar-water sauce over apples occasionally during baking. This will glaze apples and keep them from drying out.

Serve warm or chilled.

4 servings.

< Corer

Peanut Butter Pudding

Prepare as directed ——————— **1 package vanilla instant pudding**

Beat in with rotary egg beater ——— **¼ cup peanut butter**

Spoon pudding into four dessert dishes. Chill in refrigerator at least 1 hour.

4 servings.

Hot Fudge Pudding

A topsy-turvy dessert—after baking, the cake is on the top and the sauce is on the bottom.

Heat oven to 350°.

Stir together in bowl ———————
1 cup Gold Medal Flour
¾ cup sugar
2 teaspoons baking powder
¼ teaspoon salt
2 tablespoons cocoa

Stir in ———————
½ cup milk
2 tablespoons vegetable oil
1 cup chopped nuts

Spread in a square pan, 9x9x1¾ inches.

Blend in small bowl ———————
1 cup brown sugar (packed)
¼ cup cocoa

Sprinkle this mixture over top of batter.

Pour over all ——————— **1¾ cups hot water**

Bake *45 minutes.*

Serve warm or cold with milk or cream.

9 servings.

Banana Split   *Ice Cream Flower Pot*

Ice Cream Flower Pots

You will need ———————

colored small waxed paper cups
or small pottery flower pots
ice cream
chocolate shot
fresh or artificial flowers or lollipops

The paper cups can be your flower pots. Fill them with ice cream. (One pint fills 4 cups just right.) Sprinkle tops with chocolate shot.

Freeze several hours or until firm.

With a skewer, make a small hole in the center of ice cream and insert a flower or a lollipop and gumdrop leaves.

Serve immediately.

Two-tone Sundae

Kookie Kats   *Rocky Road Sundae*

Kookie Kat Sundaes

You will need —

> your favorite ice cream
> small paper or plastic dishes
> colored candy-coated milk chocolate
>   candies
> small round cookies (chocolate
>   or vanilla)

Place a big scoop of ice cream in each paper dish. This is the head for your Kookie Kat.

Use candies for eyes and mouth. For ears, push cookies into ice cream.

If you like, sprinkle on a little toasted coconut for hair.

Serve immediately.

Banana Split

The biggest and gooiest! Just like you'd order at the soda fountain.

For each serving, peel and slice in half lengthwise

> **1 banana**

Place banana halves in a shallow dish.

Top with a scoop *each* of

> **vanilla ice cream**
> **strawberry ice cream**
> **chocolate ice cream**

Spoon over ice cream

> **chocolate sauce and fruit syrups**

Top with

> **commercially prepared whipped cream**
> **fruits and nuts**

Serve immediately.

Caramel Sundae Sauce

In bottom part of double boiler, heat about 1 inch water to boiling.

Mix in top part of double boiler

> **1 package of our golden caramel frosting mix**
> **3 tablespoons soft butter**
> **2 tablespoons light corn syrup**

Stir in slowly

> **⅔ cup milk**

Place over boiling water; heat, stirring occasionally, until creamy and smooth, about 5 minutes. Cool.

Makes 2 cups sauce.

Note: Store any leftover sauce in covered container in refrigerator.

Super Caramel Sundaes

In tall sherbet glasses or in saucedishes, alternate scoops of vanilla ice cream and Caramel Sauce (above).

Freeze until serving time. If you like, top with whipped cream and garnish with pecan halves or walnut halves.

Two-tone Sundaes

Chocolate and Caramel—a favorite flavor twosome in candy. Now team up as sauces on a sundae!

In addition to the Caramel Sauce (above), prepare Chocolate Sauce (follow directions for Caramel Sauce except—substitute 1 package of our chocolate fudge flavor frosting mix for the caramel frosting mix). In tall sherbet glasses, alternate layers of vanilla ice cream with each kind of sauce.

Rocky Road Ice Cream Topping

In bottom part of double boiler, heat about 1 inch water to boiling.

Mix in top of double boiler

> 1 package of our chocolate fudge flavor frosting mix
> 3 tablespoons soft butter
> 2 tablespoons light corn syrup

Stir in slowly

> ⅔ cup milk

Place over boiling water; heat, stirring occasionally, until creamy and smooth (about 5 minutes). Cool slightly.

Stir in

> 1 cup miniature marshmallows

Serve warm over vanilla or peppermint ice cream.

Makes 2 cups sauce.

Note: Store leftover sauce in tightly covered container in the refrigerator.

Red Devil Sundae Topping

This is different and delicious. The candies make it a pretty red color.

Drain

> 1 can (8¾ ounces) crushed pineapple

Mix in saucepan

> drained pineapple
> 1 tablespoon red cinnamon candies
> 2 tablespoons light corn syrup

Simmer over medium heat, stirring constantly, until candies dissolve. Remove from heat and chill.

Serve over vanilla ice cream.

Makes about 1 cup sauce.

Confetti Pie

Crumb Crust

Crush with a rolling pin —————— | about 11 graham crackers (enough for 1 cup crumbs)

Mix in 9-inch pie pan —————— | 1 cup graham cracker crumbs
2 tablespoons sugar

Melt in small saucepan —————— | ⅓ cup butter

Mix melted butter into crumb mixture. Press crumbs firmly and evenly against bottom and sides of pie pan.

Fill with Confetti Pie Filling (below).

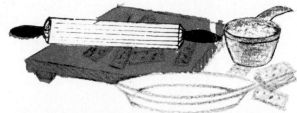

Confetti Pie Filling

Prepare filling as directed on —————— | 1 package (4 ounces) chocolate-flavored pudding and pie filling mix

Cool.

Prepare topping as directed on —————— | 1 package (2 ounces) dessert topping mix

Fold carefully into the pudding —————— | ½ of the dessert topping
1 cup multicolored miniature marshmallows
¼ cup chopped nuts, if you like

Spoon into graham cracker crust. Garnish top of pie with remaining half of the dessert topping. Sprinkle with more multicolored miniature marshmallows.

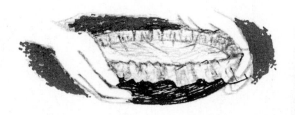

To cut pie for serving, dip knife in glass of water before cutting each piece.

Note: To prevent a film from forming on pudding as it cools, place a piece of waxed paper directly on top.

Jiffy Tarts

Confetti Pie

Strawberry Minute Pie

Strawberry Minute Pie

Prepare an 8-inch baked pie shell as directed on

1 package of our pie crust mix

Cool.

Stir in bowl until *thoroughly* dissolved

**1 package (3 ounces) strawberry-flavored gelatin
1 cup boiling water**

Add

1 package (16 ounces) frozen sweetened sliced strawberries (unthawed)

Break up berries with a fork. When fruit mixture is partially set, pour into cooled baked pie shell.

Chill in refrigerator until filling is set.

Just before serving, top with whipped cream or ice cream. Garnish with fresh strawberries, if you like.

Tart Shells

Make these for an easy company dessert.

Heat oven to 450°.

Prepare the pastry for one-crust pie as directed on

1 package of our pie crust mix

Divide dough into 6 parts.

On lightly floured board, roll out rounds of pastry with floured rolling pin. (For easier rolling, use a lightly floured cloth-covered board and rolling pin.)

Place rounds over inverted custard cups. Pinch pleats in pastry. Prick with fork and place on baking sheet. Bake *8 to 10 minutes*. Cool. Fill with your choice of Jiffy Fillings (below).

Pleat dough around custard cups like this, so pastry will fit cups.

Jiffy Fillings

1. Ice cream topped with chocolate or butterscotch sauce and chopped nuts, or topped with fresh fruit.

2. Fresh fruit topped with jam to sweeten, such as blueberries with blueberry jam or orange marmalade.

3. Cooled pudding made from a mix and topped with whipped cream or nuts.

4. Canned cherry pie filling with a topping of whipped cream.

Candies and Snacks

For fun in the kitchen and a treat besides, stir up a batch of fudge, caramel-coat big red apples, or fill a bowl with a crunchy cereal snack. Everyone loves to nibble goodies like these! And remember, a gift-wrapped box of home-made candy is a wonderful present for your teacher.

Chocolate Fudge

Mix in saucepan

> 1 cup sugar
> 1/3 cup cocoa

Stir in

> 1/4 cup butter
> 1/4 cup milk
> 1 tablespoon light corn syrup

Bring to boiling. Boil 1 minute, stirring constantly.

Remove from heat.

Add immediately

> 1 teaspoon vanilla
> 1/2 cup chopped nuts

Adding 1 cup at a time, stir in

> 2½ to 3 cups sifted confectioners' sugar

Turn into an ungreased square pan, 8x8x2 inches, and pat out with fingers. Cool.

Cut into squares.

Makes about 36 squares.

Marshmallow Fudge

Such an easy fudge to make!

Butter a square pan, 9x9x1¾ inches.

Stir in saucepan

> 1 can (6 ounces) evaporated milk
> (2/3 cup)
> 1 2/3 cups sugar
> 1/2 teaspoon salt

Cook over low heat until mixture boils. Boil 3 minutes, stirring constantly.

Remove from heat.

Add and stir until melted

> 2 cups miniature marshmallows
> 1½ packages (6 ounces each) semisweet chocolate pieces (1½ cups)

Stir in

> 1 teaspoon vanilla
> 1/2 cup chopped nuts

Pour into prepared pan. Refrigerate until firm.

Cut into squares.

Makes about 36 squares.

Opera Fudge

Butter a loaf pan, 9x5x3 inches.

In bottom part of double boiler, heat about 1 inch water to boiling.

Place in top part of double boiler

> **3 tablespoons butter**
> **3 tablespoons milk**

Set over the boiling water to melt butter.

Add and stir until blended

> **1 package of our creamy white frosting mix**

Cook over boiling water 5 minutes, stirring occasionally.

Remove from heat.

If you like, stir in

> **½ cup chopped nuts**

Pour into prepared pan and let stand until firm. (If you like, decorate with maraschino cherries.)

Cut into squares.

Makes about 32 small squares.

Creamy Chocolate Bites

Mix with fork in bowl

> **1 package of our fudge flavor frosting mix**
> **½ cup soft butter**
> **1 teaspoon vanilla**

Work mixture with hands until it forms a ball.

Dust board lightly with confectioners' sugar. Knead candy mixture about 20 times on board.

Shape in one of the following ways:

Balls—Roll candy mixture into balls about the size of walnuts. Roll each ball in chopped nuts, chocolate shot, or multicolored candies. *Makes about 48 balls.*

Slices—Mold candy mixture into 2 rolls about 1 inch thick. Roll in chopped nuts, chocolate shot, or multicolored candies. With a sharp knife, cut rolls into ½-inch slices. *Makes about 72 slices.*

Note: Store candy in tightly covered container in refrigerator.

Caramel Pralines

In bottom part of double boiler, heat about 1 inch water to boiling.

Place in top part of double boiler————— **2 tablespoons butter**
2 tablespoons plus 1 teaspoon water

Set over the boiling water to melt butter.

Add and stir until blended ————— **1 package of our golden caramel frosting mix**

Cook over boiling water 5 minutes, stirring occasionally. Remove from heat.

Stir in ————— **1 cup pecan halves**

Drop candy by teaspoonfuls onto waxed paper. Let stand until firm.

Makes about 36 candies.

Peanut Butter Creams

Beat with rotary egg beater in bowl ————— **1 egg**

Beat in until smooth ————— **⅓ cup peanut butter**
1 tablespoon soft butter
½ teaspoon vanilla
⅛ teaspoon salt
1 cup sifted confectioners' sugar

Stir in ————— **1 cup more sifted confectioners' sugar**

Shape mixture into tiny balls. (More confectioners' sugar may be added to make candy firm enough to handle.)

Roll each ball in ————— **¾ cup finely chopped salted peanuts**

Place on waxed paper and refrigerate until firm.

Makes about 36 candies.

Chocolate Coconut Drops

Heat oven to 350°.

In bottom part of double boiler, heat about 1 inch water to boiling.

Place in top part of double boiler — **2 squares unsweetened chocolate (2 ounces)**

Set over the boiling water to melt chocolate. Remove from heat.

Stir in — **1 can (15 ounces) sweetened condensed milk**
7 ounces (2 cups) flaked coconut (packed)
½ cup chopped nuts

Drop by rounded teaspoonfuls onto ungreased baking sheet.

Place in oven; *turn off heat at once.* Leave in oven 15 to 20 minutes, or until candy has a glazed appearance. Remove from baking sheet while warm.

Makes about 48 drops.

Pictured below: 1—Opera Fudge; 2—Caramel Pralines; 3, 5, 8—Creamy Chocolate Bites; 4—Chocolate Fudge; 6—Peanut Butter Creams; 7—Chocolate Coconut Drops

Cereal Marshmallow Bars

Butter a square pan, 9x9x1¾ inches, and a large bowl.

Mix in bowl

> **4 cups Kix or Cheerios**
> **½ cup shredded or flaked coconut**
> **¼ cup coarsely chopped nuts**

In bottom part of double boiler, heat about 1 inch water to boiling.

Place in top part of double boiler

> **3 tablespoons butter or margarine**
> **4 cups miniature marshmallows**

Set over the boiling water and stir until marshmallows are melted.

Pour marshmallow mixture over cereal. Stir gently to coat cereal.

Using rubber scraper, turn into prepared pan and pat out with fingers greased with butter.

Cool. Cut into bars.

Makes about 27 bars.

Carameled Kix

Butter a square pan, 9x9x1¾ inches.

Measure into large buttered bowl

> **5 cups Kix**

In bottom part of double boiler, heat about 1 inch water to boiling.

Place in top part of double boiler

> **26 caramels (8 ounces)**
> **2 tablespoons water**

Set over the boiling water until caramels are melted.

Pour caramel mixture over Kix and stir gently to coat cereal.

Using rubber scraper, turn caramel mixture into prepared pan and pat out with fingers lightly greased with butter. Refrigerate until firm.

Cut into bars.

Makes about 24 bars.

Kix Comets

Measure into large bowl

> **5 cups Kix**

In bottom part of double boiler, heat about 1 inch water to boiling.

Place in top part of double boiler

> **1 package (6 ounces) semisweet chocolate pieces**

Set over the boiling water until melted.

Pour chocolate mixture over Kix and stir gently to coat cereal.

Form into cone shapes on waxed paper. Chill in refrigerator until firm, at least 2 hours.

Makes about 60 pieces.

Wheaties Ting-a-Lings

In bottom part of double boiler, heat about 1 inch water to boiling.

Place in top part of double boiler

> **2 packages (6 ounces each) semisweet chocolate pieces**

Set over the boiling water until melted.

Remove top part of double boiler from heat. Let chocolate cool.

Gently stir in

> **4 cups Wheaties**

Drop by tablespoonfuls onto waxed paper. Chill in refrigerator until chocolate is set, about 2 hours.

Makes about 42 pieces.

Pictured at right: Pink Popcorn Balls, Carameled Kix, Cereal Marshmallow Bars, Wheaties Ting-a-Lings, Chocolate-Caramel Apples

Chocolate-Caramel Apples

Wash and dry ————————————————— 6 medium apples

Stick a wooden skewer into stem end of each apple.

Place in each of 6 mounds, a few inches apart,
on waxed paper ————————————————— 1 tablespoon chopped nuts

In bottom part of double boiler, heat about 1 inch water to boiling.

Place in top part of double boiler ————————
1 package (14 ounces) caramels (49)
2 tablespoons hot water
¼ cup semisweet chocolate pieces

Set over the boiling water and stir until caramels and chocolate are melted.

Remove double boiler from heat, keeping top part over hot water.

With a knife or spatula, spread apples with caramel mixture.

Place each caramel-coated apple on a mound of nuts. If you like, sprinkle any remaining nuts around skewers.

Makes 6 chocolate-caramel apples.

Note: If caramel mixture hardens while spreading apples, place double boiler over heat and bring water to boiling again.

Holding each apple over pan, spread with caramel mixture.

Then place in mound of nuts.

Pink Popcorn Balls

Fun to make on a Sunday afternoon.
Our young testers loved these—so did their
mothers and fathers!

Place in large buttered bowl

7 cups popped popcorn

In bottom part of double boiler, heat about 1 inch water to boiling.

Place in top part of double boiler

3 cups miniature marshmallows
2 tablespoons butter
¼ teaspoon salt

Set over the boiling water and stir until marshmallows are melted.

Tint pink by adding

a few drops of red food coloring

Pour marshmallow mixture over popcorn and stir gently to coat.

Grease hands well with butter and quickly shape popcorn into 10 medium-sized balls.

Makes 10 popcorn balls.

"The pink made the popcorn pretty."—Joan

Marguerites

A favorite with your mother or grandmother
when she was a young girl.

Heat oven to 400°.

Arrange on baking sheet

24 soda crackers

Beat with rotary egg beater or electric mixer just until frothy

2 egg whites (see page 90)

Gradually beat in

¼ cup sugar

Continue beating until stiff peaks form.

Stir in

¼ teaspoon vanilla
½ cup chopped nuts, if you like

Spoon this meringue onto crackers, spreading to edge of each cracker.

Bake *6 to 8 minutes,* or just until golden brown. Do not overbake!

Beat egg whites until peaks are stiff—test by pulling beater up like this.

Note: Next time your mother is frosting a cake with our packaged fluffy white frosting, you can use any extra for a few Speedy Marguerites. Just add a few nuts to frosting; spread on soda crackers. Bake as directed above.

Nuts 'n Bolts

Heat oven to 250°.

Mix in large baking pan

- 1 cup Kix
- 1 cup Cheerios
- 1 cup thin pretzel sticks
- ½ cup salted peanuts or mixed nuts

Melt in small saucepan

- 3 tablespoons butter

Stir in

- ¼ teaspoon Worcestershire sauce
- ⅛ teaspoon garlic salt
- ⅛ teaspoon celery salt

Pour butter mixture over cereals. Stir and salt lightly.

Bake *30 minutes*, stirring carefully with wooden spoon several times.

Makes about 3 cups.

Cinnamon Crunchies

Sweet and salty—so good for nibbling.

Heat oven to 325°.

Butter a baking sheet.

In small bowl, beat with rotary egg beater until foamy

- 1 egg white (see page 90)

Mix in

- ½ cup sugar
- ¼ teaspoon salt
- ¼ teaspoon cinnamon

Stir in

- 3 cups Twinkles
- ½ cup chopped nuts

Mix well. Spread on prepared baking sheet.

Bake *20 minutes*.

Cool slightly. Remove from baking sheet with spatula.

Break into pieces.

Special Occasions

Holidays and family celebrations call for especially good things to eat. Try the bright ideas and recipes in this chapter for Valentine's Day, Halloween, or birthday parties. See how proud you'll be when you surprise Mom or Dad with a dinner you've cooked all by yourself.

Around-the-Year Cupcakes

*It's fun to celebrate a holiday or birthday with cupcakes that match the month.
Here are some bright and easy ideas for each month of the year.
Take your choice—or make up your own ideas.*

Prepare and bake cupcakes as directed on ▬▬▬ **1 package of any of our layer cake mixes except marble**

Prepare frosting as directed on ▬▬▬ **1 package of our fluffy white frosting mix**

Frost and decorate cooled cupcakes, following the directions for the month you choose.

January—Jolly Snowmen

Frost cupcakes with white frosting.

Make each snowman, as shown, with 1 large marshmallow, 3 miniature marshmallows, and 2 toothpicks. Use a rounded slice from a 1-inch gumdrop for the hat. With frosting, fasten on 2 cinnamon candy buttons. Stick a snowman on top of each cupcake.

February—Red Hatchets

Add 1 or 2 drops only of blue food coloring to the white frosting. Frost cupcakes with the light blue frosting.

Cut each hatchet (about 3½ inches long) from red construction paper. Stick into a cupcake at an angle.

March—Shamrocks

Add 1 or 2 drops only of green food coloring to the white frosting. Frost cupcakes with the light green frosting.

Slice a 1-inch green gumdrop as shown. Arrange 3 pieces on cupcake to form a shamrock. Cut out the stem from remaining large slice. Repeat for other cupcakes.

April—Rainy-day Umbrellas

Add 1 or 2 drops only of yellow food coloring to the white frosting. Frost cupcakes with the yellow frosting.

For top of each umbrella, place a candied fruit slice on cupcake, as shown. For handle, cut a strip from gumdrop stick; shape into a "J." Place beneath umbrella top.

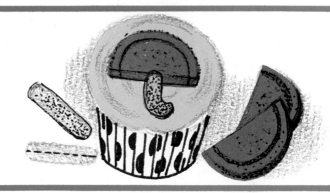

May—Flower Baskets

Frost cupcakes with white frosting.

With scissors, snip the wide part of a small gumdrop into 6 sections, as shown—*do not cut through.* Carefully spread gumdrop "petals" apart and place sugared side up on each cupcake. Slice green gumdrop for stem and leaves. Add a colored pipe cleaner for basket handle.

June—Gay Tulips

Add 1 or 2 drops only of green food coloring to the white frosting. Frost cupcakes with the light green frosting.

Place a colored 1-inch gumdrop on end of toothpick and stick into each cupcake, as shown. For leaves, cut a green candied fruit slice into pie-shaped pieces; place around "stem."

Fourth of July—Firecrackers

Add 1 or 2 drops only of blue food coloring to the white frosting. Frost cupcakes with the light blue frosting.

Stick 3 small red candles upright into each cupcake, as shown.

August—Summer Daisies

Frost cupcakes with white frosting.

Place 1 semisweet chocolate piece in center of each cupcake.

For petals, use yellow or pink pillow mints.

September—Apples for the Teacher

Add 1 or 2 drops only of red food coloring to the white frosting. Frost cupcakes with the pink frosting.

Cut stem of each maraschino cherry so that it is only about ½ inch long. Place one on each cupcake, as shown.

October—Halloween Cats

Add 1 or 2 drops of red and 1 or 2 drops of yellow food coloring to the white frosting. Frost cupcakes with the orange frosting.

Slice a 1-inch black gumdrop into 3 pieces, as shown. Use small rounded end slice for head; use largest slice for body. Cut ears and tail from third slice, as shown. Form a cat on cupcake with gumdrop pieces. Repeat for other cupcakes.

November—Pumpkins

Frost cupcakes with white frosting.

To make each pumpkin, cut a small slit in top of a 1-inch orange gumdrop. Stick a small piece of a green gumdrop in slit for stem. Place a pumpkin in center of each cupcake.

December—Christmas Bells

Frost cupcakes with white frosting.

Cut a green candied fruit slice, as shown. On cupcake, form a bow with the pie-shaped pieces; add streamers with the rectangular slices.

For bell, cut maraschino cherry in half. Place cut side down at end of streamers on cupcake. Repeat for other cupcakes.

Heart Cake

A beautiful surprise for Valentine's Day—or any special day. See the Mother's Day Heart Cake on page 142.

Grease and flour one square pan, 8x8x2 inches, and one round layer pan, 8x1½ inches.

Prepare cake batter as directed on ———

1 package of our white cake mix

Divide batter between the prepared pans.

Bake square layer *30 to 35 minutes,* round layer *35 to 40 minutes,* or until toothpick stuck in center comes out clean. Cool as directed on package.

To make heart-shaped cake: Place square cake on large tray with one point toward you. Cut round layer in half. Place each half with cut edge against top sides of the square to form heart.

Prepare frosting as directed on ———

1 package of our fluffy white frosting mix

Tint frosting pink with a few drops of red food coloring.

Frost cake, being sure to cover top of cake well, especially over the cut sections. Decorate with red cinnamon candies.

Valentine's Party

Silhouette Sandwiches (page 40)
Celery Curls (page 50)
Cocoa Continental with Pink Whipped Cream
(page 23)
Heart Cake

Easter Eggs—Before and After

Dye them, paint them, trim them with paper and lace, buttons and braids, ribbons and feathers. There is no end to the pretty or comically decorated Easter eggs you can make. All you need is a paintbrush or crayons, glue, and bits of trimmings saved from Christmas packages or Mother's sewing box—or found in the dime store.

First, hard cook the eggs (page 77).

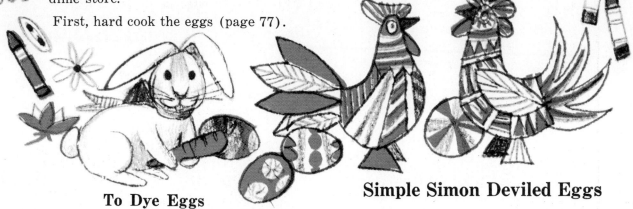

To Dye Eggs

Prepare Easter egg dyes as directed on package, or use a few drops of food coloring in custard cups or muffin tins with enough hot water to cover egg. With a tablespoon, dip eggs one by one into dye. Let stand, turning occasionally until evenly colored. Lift out egg and place on paper towels or in carton to dry.

Variations on Dyeing Eggs

Cut designs from cellophane or adhesive tape and paste on eggs before dipping in dye. Remove tape when dry for white designs.

Easter egg place cards for an Easter Sunday meal can be made by writing each guest's name on egg with crayon before dyeing.

To Decorate Colored Eggs

Be imaginative! Glue on your choice of pretty trims—rickrack, buttons, bows, or velvet ribbon and tiny artificial flowers. (Pictured on page 127.)

Simple Simon Deviled Eggs

After Easter, you can eat some of your Easter eggs this zippy way.

Remove shells from

6 hard-cooked eggs

Slice eggs in half lengthwise.

With a teaspoon, remove egg yolks and place in mixing bowl.

Mash

egg yolks

Mix in

3 tablespoons mayonnaise
2 tablespoons hot dog relish
¼ teaspoon salt

Fill center of egg whites with the egg yolk mixture.

Sprinkle paprika over the egg. Chill and serve.

6 servings.

Easter Breakfast

Easter Egg Place Cards
Funny Bunny Biscuits
Individual Boxes of Cereal

(Arrange an Easter Egg, Funny Bunny Biscuit, and box of cereal in a pretty little basket. Set one basket on each person's plate at the breakfast table.)

Funny Bunny Biscuits

Heat oven to 450°.

Prepare Rolled Biscuits (page 31) as directed except—do not bake.

Place 8 biscuits on ungreased baking sheet. Cut remaining biscuits in half; lengthen halves to form ears.

Press ears to whole biscuit to form bunny head.

Press in raisins for eyes, a candied cherry for a nose, and slivered almonds for whiskers.

Bake *10 to 12 minutes.*

If you like, frost the ears with a mixture of ½ cup sifted confectioners' sugar and 1 tablespoon milk tinted pink with red food coloring.

Makes 8 biscuits.

Your bunny biscuits will look like this.

Peter Rabbit Cake

Make this for a special Easter dinner dessert.

Bake cake batter in oblong pan, 13x9½x2 inches, as directed on

> 1 package of any of our layer cake mixes except marble

Frost cooled cake in pan with

> Quick Fudge Frosting (page 104) or our chocolate fudge flavor frosting mix

Cut into 15 squares and remove from pan.

Make marshmallow bunny face as directed below on each square piece of cake.

Snip marshmallow into two flat circles with scissors and place one on cake for bunny face.

Snip other half of marshmallow for bunny ears.

With a toothpick dipped in food coloring, draw a bunny face.

Christmas Tree Cake

Black Cat Cookies

Jack-o'-Lantern Cake

Drum Cake

Drum Cake

To celebrate the Fourth of July, make a cake for the family picnic.

Bake cake batter in round layer pans
as directed on **1 package of our devils food cake mix**

Prepare frosting as directed on **1 package of our fluffy white frosting mix**

Frost cooled cake.

On sides of cake, press into frosting at angles **striped peppermint candy sticks**

Place a big red maraschino cherry at ends of sticks. If you like, cross two candy sticks on top of cake for drumsticks.

Picnic in the Park
Cold Fried Drumsticks (page 66)
Potato Chips   Relishes (pages 50-51)
Bread-and-Butter Sandwiches
Drum Cake

Black Cat Cookies

Tricky treats for Halloween.

Make Sparkling Sugar Cookies (page 86).

As soon as cookies come from oven, place a chocolate peppermint wafer in the center of each.

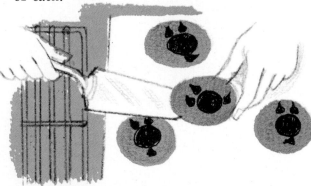

Place 2 semisweet chocolate pieces next to mint for head, 1 piece for tail. Lift onto cooling rack as chocolate melts.

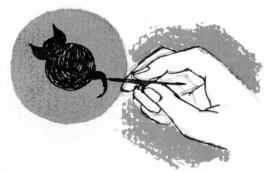

With toothpick, shape melted chocolate pieces into head and tail of a cat.

Jack-o'-Lantern Cake

A spooky spice cake for your Halloween party.

Bake cake batter in round layer pans as directed on

1 package of our spice cake mix

Prepare frosting as directed on

1 package of our fluffy white frosting mix

Tint orange with several drops *each* of red and yellow food coloring.

Frost cooled cake.

Make a jack-o'-lantern face with

flat black jelly candies and candy corn

Note: To make cake as pictured (page 134), prepare 2 packages of our fluffy white frosting mix; tint orange with several drops *each* of red and yellow food coloring. Frost cake, rounding the sides and top to resemble a pumpkin.

Halloween Party

Jack-o'-Lantern Cake
or
Black Cat Cookies
Jack Frost Warmer
(page 23)

Christmas Snacks for Friends
Pink Popcorn Balls (page 125)
Christmas Tree Cake
Cocoa Continental (page 23)

Christmas Tree Cake

Cut the cake and see each piece sparkle with candy Christmas lights.

Grease and flour an oblong pan, 13x9½x2 inches.

Prepare cake batter as directed on ══════ | 1 package of our white or yellow cake mix

Pour batter into prepared pan.

Sprinkle batter with ══════════════════ | 2 tablespoons green decorators' sugar
2 tablespoons multicolored tiny decorators' candies

Swirl through batter with spatula. Bake as directed on package.

Cover large tray or cardboard with aluminum foil. Cut cooled cake as shown in diagram.

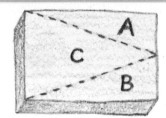

Prepare frosting as directed on ══════ | 1 package of our fluffy white frosting mix

Tint frosting light green with a few drops of food coloring.

Put cake pieces A and B on tray to make shape of a tree. Frost. Place piece C on top; frost top and sides, making strokes through frosting to resemble branches.

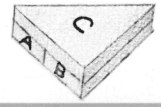

Sprinkle entire cake with ══════ | green decorators' sugar

To make trunk, insert in bottom of cake ══ | 3 candy canes

Place on cake ══════ | red candles

"Big Top" Party

For your little brother's or sister's friends or for your own group—a Saturday afternoon "Big Top" Party is almost as much fun as front row seats at a real-life circus.

Invitations can be tickets cut from pink construction paper or cardboard. Write on each invitation with colored crayon:

ADMIT ONE to Mary Jones' Circus Saturday, May 8 at 3 P.M.

To make a circus-tent table: Cut wide strips of bright crepe paper and arrange them on the cloth in a pinwheel pattern from the center of the table. Or have someone help you tie crepe paper streamers from the light fixture above the dining room table to the back of each chair.

Place cards may be balloons tied to each chair and labeled with the name of each guest. Use a felt ink marker or nail polish for writing on balloons. The Parade Cake is your centerpiece. Set it on a pedestal cake plate or a sturdy up-turned box covered with aluminum foil so that everyone can see it.

Popcorn Ball Clowns are favors at each place. Prepare Pink Popcorn Balls (page 125). To make clown faces, press small candies and nuts onto popcorn balls. Attach ears of candied fruit slices with toothpicks. Stick toothpick into top of popcorn ball; place an ice cream cone upside down over toothpick for hat. (Press gumdrop slices onto cone, if you like.) A base and a bow tie may be made from colored construction paper.

Circus Party Refreshments

Circus Parade Cake
Chocolate, Strawberry, or Vanilla Ice Cream
Pink Lemonade (page 16)

Circus Parade Cake

You're the ringmaster—make your own animals and march them around the cake.

Bake cake batter in round layer pans as directed on ———————— | **1 package of any of our layer cake mixes except marble**

Prepare frosting as directed on ———————— | **1 package of our fluffy white frosting mix**

Frost cooled cake. Reserve a small amount of frosting for sticking faces on Cooky-and-Candy Animals (below).

To make Cooky-and-Candy Animals: On a tray or counter top, arrange your choice of cookies, candies, popcorn, peanuts, pretzels, or marshmallows to look like any animal you like. "Glue" on faces with reserved frosting, as necessary. (Cut gumdrops will stick without frosting.)

When you've made an animal you like, pick up the pieces and press onto side of cake. Decorate top of cake with colored gumdrops and candles.

Moon Menu

Blast-off Burgers (Sloppy Joes, page 46)
Energy Capsules (stuffed olives)
Energy Sticks (carrot sticks)
Weightless Wafers (potato chips)
Crater Sundaes
Milky Way Punch (milk)

Planet Hopping Party

Invite your friends to join you for a blast-off from Cape "Brown" (your own last name) and spend an afternoon in a make-believe land of outer space.

For invitations, cut spaceships from colored construction paper. Write with colored crayon:

INTERPLANETARY MESSAGE.... ENTER THE ATMOSPHERE FROM JERRY BROWN'S LAUNCHING PAD —SATURDAY, JUNE 2 --- 12 NOON
P.S. RETURN SIGNAL REQUESTED

To make an outer-space refreshment table: Paste gummed gold and silver stars on blue cloth or crepe paper. This is your tablecloth. Use a large globe of the world as the centerpiece. Set the table with solid-colored paper plates and cups, and plastic forks.

For satellite place cards, stick multicolored toothpicks into all sides of a big marshmallow. Print the name of each guest on a piece of construction paper. Make up space names such as Mary from Mars, Peter from Pluto, Sally from Saturn, Mike from Mercury. Tape each piece of paper onto a satellite.

Crater Sundaes

You will need

chocolate ice cream
marshmallow creme
chopped nuts
semisweet chocolate pieces

Place a large scoop of ice cream into each sauce-dish. Press a hole in top of each ice cream mountain to make a "crater." Fill with marshmallow creme. Sprinkle with nuts and chocolate pieces.

Use two spoons, held tip to tip, to press hole in ice cream. Work quickly so ice cream won't melt.

Feast for Father

Dad will be so very pleased and proud if his Father's Day or birthday dinner is cooked by you! Switch jobs with Mother and let her be your assistant for such a special occasion. She'll be happy to set the table, make the coffee, and give any other help needed with these recipes for a family of four.

Oven-fried Drumsticks (page 66)
Baked Potatoes (page 61)
Buttered Succotash
Tossed Green Salad (page 53)
Ice Cream
Name Cake (page 102)
Milk   Coffee

It's great fun to go shopping with Mother for the groceries that you are going to use. First, jot down a list of the food needed. Mother will help you check in the kitchen to see what is already on hand.

Kitchen Check List

eggs	flour
milk	salt
butter	pepper
soft shortening	dry mustard
vegetable oil	paprika
vinegar	lemon or lemon juice
	coffee

You May Need to Buy

chicken legs-you'll need 2 pounds	carrots
	celery
baking potatoes-you'll need 4 medium	succotash-frozen or canned
head lettuce	ice cream
radishes	

1 package of our layer cake mix-chocolate or spice cake would be a good choice for Dad

1 package of our creamy-type frosting mix—choose a light-colored one for Name Cake

semisweet chocolate pieces

small birthday candles-if the occasion is Dad's birthday

Helpful Hints for Cooking This Dinner:

1. *Plan ahead.* Look over your recipes. Bake and frost Name Cake the day before your dinner, or in the morning. This way, you needn't bother with the cake while busy cooking dinner. Your salad dressing can be mixed in a jar, then refrigerated until needed.

2. *About 1¼ hours before you plan to serve dinner,* heat oven to 425°. Scrub and prick potatoes and place in oven—they bake for about 1 hour in a 425° oven. Flour the chicken legs as directed in the recipe; place in the oven with the potatoes.

3. *While dinner bakes,* tear lettuce for salad into bowl. Slice vegetables and add; place bowl in refrigerator. (It's best to toss a salad with the dressing just before serving.)

4. *Cook succotash.* Use frozen or canned succotash and cook as directed on package or can.

5. *Toss salad;* place bowl on table.

6. *When all the food is cooked,* you're ready to take your dinner to the table. With hot pads, carefully remove chicken and potatoes from oven. Squeeze open potatoes as directed in your recipe. Place chicken and potatoes on platter, succotash in a bowl; carry to the table.

Mother's Day Dinner

This is *your* big dinner of the year. And here's what to cook and how to do it!

"Ham" Loaf Hawaiian (page 68)
Fluffy Mashed Potatoes
Buttered Green Beans
Lettuce Wedge Salad (page 52)
Heart Cake (page 131)
Milk   Coffee

Dad can pitch in to make the coffee. Let your brother or sister have a part in this dinner, too—setting the table would be a fine job.

(If you are just learning how to cook, wait until another year to prepare this complete dinner. Right now, Mother would be delighted if you'd bake the Heart Cake for her day.)

Step by Step to Dinner for Four

1. *On the Saturday before Mother's Day,* bake and frost Heart Cake. Store cake loosely covered with aluminum foil.

2. *On Sunday,* set the table (page 14). For a centerpiece, fill a low vase with your favorite flowers. Decorate Heart Cake with red cinnamon candies, as shown.

3. *About 1 hour before you are planning to serve dinner,* cut lettuce wedges and place on small plates; trim with radishes and cucumber slices. Refrigerate.

4. *About 35 minutes before dinnertime,* heat oven to 375°.

5. *Prepare "Ham" Loaf* as directed in your recipe. It bakes for 20 minutes. Meanwhile, cook a 10-ounce package of frozen green beans as directed on package.

6. *Pour water and milk* into glasses and set on the table.

7. *While beans are cooking,* prepare our mashed Potato Buds as directed on package for 4 servings. Cover to keep warm.

8. *Remove salads* from refrigerator. Pour your favorite bottled salad dressing over each lettuce wedge. Place on table, one salad plate to the left of each fork.

9. *With hot pads,* remove the "Ham" Loaf from oven. Drain beans; dot with butter. Arrange beans on platter or in baking dish with "Ham" Loaf. Spoon potatoes into a serving bowl; dot with butter.

10. DINNER IS READY!
Don't forget to leave Mother's kitchen, after the meal, as neat and clean as you found it.

Surprise Breakfast

Have you ever wished you could get up some morning to fix breakfast for the whole family? You can, and it's lots of fun! Try this exciting adventure on Mother's Day or a birthday, or on a Sunday morning when you just want to let Mother and Dad sleep a little later than usual.

Cinnamon Puffs

See these pictured on page 23.

Heat oven to 450°.

Prepare Rolled Biscuits (page 31) as directed except—after kneading, divide dough into 16 parts. Roll each part into a smooth ball.

Place balls on ungreased baking sheet.

Bake *10 to 12 minutes.*

Melt in small skillet

⅓ **cup butter**

Mix in small bowl

½ **cup sugar**
2 teaspoons cinnamon

While biscuits are warm, remove from sheet and roll each in melted butter; then roll in the cinnamon-sugar mixture.

Makes 16 puffs.

Chilled Orange Juice
Bowls of Cereal topped with Fruit
Cinnamon Puffs
Cocoa Continental (page 23)

Here's the Way for an Easy Breakfast

1. *Plan ahead.* It's a good idea to have the orange juice chilling in the refrigerator, all ready to serve. You can use frozen, canned, or fresh orange juice.

2. *First thing in the morning,* set the table or breakfast bar.

3. *Choose your favorite cereal;* pour into bowls and set aside.

4. *Heat oven to 450°.*

5. *Prepare Cocoa Continental* as directed in recipe. Cover pan to keep warm. (You will need to reheat cocoa just before serving.)

6. *Prepare and bake* Cinnamon Puffs.

7. *While puffs bake,* pour orange juice into glasses. Pour milk for cereal into pitcher. Place on table.

8. *Top cereal with fruit*—strawberries or sliced bananas would taste good. Place on table.

9. *When puffs are done,* remove from sheet and roll in butter and sugar mixture as directed in the recipe. Serve these spicy puffs in a basket or on a plate covered with a napkin.

10. *Reheat and pour cocoa.* Call the family.

Summer Fun

Vacation time is here again with long sunny days for riding your bike, cooking out of doors, and hiking in the woods. Girls will enjoy giving a tea party on the porch or under a shady tree; boys will want to camp out in a tent. And, of course, everybody loves a picnic!

Cook Outdoors

To cook outdoors, you'll need a fire of some sort. First check with Mom or Dad to see if it is all right for you to have one. And it's a good idea if Dad is along to give you a hand and to make sure "safety first" is always the rule.

Perhaps you'll cook on Dad's barbecue grill—he'll be glad to light the charcoal for you. Or, build a fire in a backyard or park fireplace.

Sometimes you can cook over a campfire. It's easy—and safe—if you remember to:

1. Select an open spot for your fire—clear away leaves, wood, and grass. Don't build a fire under trees or near shrubs.

2. Build a small fire.

3. Never leave a fire without someone to watch over it.

4. Keep water and dirt nearby for putting out the fire.

5. Don't play with fire! Keep matches in a safe place at all times.

Building the Campfire: The Hunter's Fire is easy and gives a steady heat. To build it, lay 2 green logs in a V-shape, about 7 inches apart at one end and 4 inches apart at the other. The wider opening should face the wind.

Build a "starter" fire between the logs and then add fuel as you need it. For best results, you should let the fire burn down to hot coals before you start to cook.

Pots and skillets can be set on the logs near the narrow end.

Note to Outdoor Cooks

Cooking time over an open fire varies, depending on how hot your fire is and how well it is controlled. Cook food until it is done the way you like to eat it.

From left to right: Frank-a-Bobs, Kabobs, Peanut Butter Pups, Make-believe Angel Food

Best Basics for Outdoor Chefs

Roasted Wieners

Of all the foods to cook outdoors, this is the easiest and the most fun.

Start with a stick that's green so it won't burn, and one just heavy enough so it won't bend with the wiener. A forked stick is really best. Whittle the stick to a point or points; slide on a wiener. Turn over the hot coals of a low fire until well browned. Toast a roll also on a stick. Serve all with plenty of mustard or catsup. Or for a special treat, try one of the following variations:

Frank-a-Bobs

Cut each frank into 5 pieces. Alternate on skewer or thin stick with pineapple chunks; brush with vegetable oil. Broil over hot coals, turning until browned. Serve on toasted frankfurter rolls.

Peanut Butter Pups

Split frankfurters lengthwise, not cutting all the way through. Spread cut surfaces with peanut butter. Wrap with a strip of bacon, anchoring with toothpicks at each end. Cook on a stick or on a grill over hot coals, turning until bacon is crisp. Remove toothpicks.

Woodsman Burgers

Shape 1 pound ground beef into 4 or 5 patties; sprinkle with salt. Place on grill 4 to 6 inches from hot coals. (For campfire cooking, place patties in squares of heavy-duty aluminum foil and place directly on top of hot coals.) Cook 15 to 20 minutes or until done, turning once.

Doughboys

You can even "bake" bread outdoors—at a picnic, on a camping trip, or in your own backyard.

Pour several cups of Bisquick into a plastic bag. Set bag upright. Roll down sides to make a cuff. With end of thin peeled green stick, make a "well" in center of Bisquick.

For each Doughboy, pour in about 1 tablespoon milk or water. Stir gently with stick until liquid picks up enough dough to form a soft ball around end of stick.

Dip your hands in Bisquick to prevent sticking, then remove the ball of dough from stick. Roll between hands into a strip, about the width of your little finger, 4 or 5 inches long.

Wind strip around the stick, pinching tightly at each end to hold it onto stick.

Bake over hot coals, turning to bake evenly. With a good bed of coals, Doughboys bake in just a few minutes and easily slip off stick.

Fill hollow center with strip of cheese, cooked meat, or spoon in jelly or jam. Eat piping hot.

Wind the dough around the stick like this.

Kabobs

This exciting dish comes from the Near East, where mountain dwellers first roasted their meat on sword blades over an outdoor fire.

Find a long green stick about as thick as a lead pencil; sharpen the thin end. This is your handmade skewer. (You can use a real skewer, if you like.)

Cut into 1-inch pieces

> ¼ pound beef sirloin

Cut in quarters and peel

> 1 onion

Cut in quarters

> 1 tomato

Push the meat, onion, and tomato alternately on the stick. Or, try an apple instead of tomato for variety. Broil by holding close to hot coals, turning constantly. Cook until meat is brown and vegetables are tender.

Makes 1 kabob for 1 dinner.

Scout Franks and Beans

Empty into a heavy skillet

> 1 can (1 pound) baked beans

Slice

> 8 frankfurters

Place on top of beans. Set on grill over coals and heat until steaming hot.

4 to 6 servings.

Coffee Can Stew with Dumplings

Season lightly with salt and pepper

> 1 pound ground beef

Divide into 4 patties.

Grease four 1-pound cans—the kind used for coffee is best.

Place in each can

> 1 meat patty
> 3 or 4 thin strips of carrot
> 3 slices tomato
> ½ cup drained whole kernel corn

Dot with butter. Season with salt and pepper. Cover each can tightly with heavy-duty aluminum foil, molding outer edges firmly against can. Place on grill; cook 20 to 30 minutes.

Prepare dough for Dumplings as directed on Bisquick package.

With hot pads, remove foil covers from cans; drop small spoonfuls of dough into each can. Cover again with foil; cook 15 to 20 minutes longer. Do not peek!

4 servings.

Angels' Halos

Make-believe Angel Food

You will need

> marshmallows
> large glazed doughnuts

You will need

> day-old unsliced bread
> sweetened condensed milk
> flaked coconut

Place a marshmallow into hole of each doughnut. Run pointed green stick or picnic skewer through doughnut and marshmallow.

Toast over hot coals of your charcoal grill or campfire.

Turn frequently to toast marshmallow a golden brown and heat doughnut thoroughly.

"We had these for dessert after a hamburger meal."—Carol

Cut bread into 2-inch slices; remove crusts. Cut slices into 2-inch squares.

Run pointed green stick or picnic skewer through bread so that it is steady.

Dip bread on stick in the condensed milk.

Immediately coat with coconut.

Toast over hot coals of your charcoal grill or campfire until coconut is brown and crunchy.

S'mores

They get this name because they make you want some more.

You will need

> milk chocolate candy bars
> graham crackers
> marshmallows

For each S'more, place 4 squares of a milk chocolate candy bar on a graham cracker.

Toast a marshmallow over the coals of your charcoal grill or campfire. Slip it onto the chocolate and top with a second graham cracker.

Picnic with a Pal

Two friends and two lunchboxes team up for a really good outing. Each person brings half the lunch, and it's a swap!

Lunchbox I
Vacuum Bottle of Hot Creamy Chicken-Vegetable Soup (page 80)

Two Bags of Corn Chips
Lumberjack Cookies (page 95)

Lunchbox II
Vacuum Bottle of Lemonade (page 16)
Two Hobo Sandwiches (below)
A Big Apple and an Orange

Hobo Sandwich

For each sandwich, slice and butter ——— | 1 small French loaf or frankfurter bun

Spread with prepared mustard.

Place between bread ——— | 1 slice American cheese
1 slice Swiss cheese, if you like
1 slice salami, bologna, or boiled ham

Leave whole or cut in half.

Note: Carry pickles, tomatoes, and lettuce to picnic in plastic dish or bag. Tuck into sandwich just before eating.

Peanut Butter Hobo

For each serving, slice and butter ——— | 1 small French loaf or frankfurter roll

Spread with ——— | peanut butter

Place between bread ——— | thin slices of orange and banana

Pitch a Tent, Have Lunch

Your tent is an old blanket hung over
the clothesline. There are many wonderful things
to do in a tent. But come noontime,
it's just the place for a picnic lunch.

Flying Saucer Picnic: For each lunch, wrap up a package
of Three-in-One Sandwiches (page 41) and place on a paper
plate. Add a pile of potato chips and a juicy plum or pear
and grapes. Tuck in a paper napkin. Cover the plate with
another plate—turned upside down. Tape top to bottom so it
will be easy to carry. Store in refrigerator until lunchtime.

For drinks, chill individual-sized cans of tomato juice (not concentrate).

Capsule Sundaes: For each, spoon vanilla ice cream into
a paper cup. Top with your favorite sundae sauce,
a little whipped cream, and a big red cherry,
if you like. Wrap a piece of aluminum foil around cup
to seal in your sundae. Freeze. At noon, carry lunch
out to your tent.

Hit the Trail with a Nosebag Lunch

Not much to carry, but energy packed!

Can of Vienna Sausages
Bread-and-Butter Sandwiches
in Foil
Hard-cooked Eggs (page 77)
Packets of Salt
Tiny Boxes of Raisins

Outdoor Tea Party

Choose a lovely summer day; then perhaps you can have your party on the porch or patio, or under a big shade tree. Ask your best friends to join you in the early afternoon.

Plate of
Party Sandwiches (page 39)
Strawberry Cooler
Lemon Shiver

Strawberry Cooler

As ice cubes melt, this drink becomes a sparkling pink punch. See it pictured on page 17.

Mix

> 1 package (1 ounce) strawberry-flavored instant soft drink mix
> ⅔ cup sugar
> 3 cups water

Pour into divided ice cube tray.

Place one whole strawberry in each cube. Freeze.

To serve, place several cubes in each glass.

Fill glass with

> lemon-lime carbonated beverage

6 servings.

Lemon Shiver

Make this ice cream in the morning, so it will be frozen and ready for your mid-afternoon snack.

In medium-sized bowl, beat with rotary egg beater until thick

> 2 eggs

Beat in

> ½ cup sugar
> ¼ cup light corn syrup

Add

> 1 teaspoon grated lemon peel
> juice of 1 lemon
> juice of 1 orange
> 1 cup cream
> ½ cup milk

Beat well. Pour into undivided ice cube tray. Freeze until the mixture is "mushy."

Pour mixture back into the bowl and beat again. Then return mixture to the ice cube tray and refreeze until solid.

Makes 1 quart.

Index